STEVE K. RICHMOND

W⚙RKING SMART

Success in
Maintenance,
Asset Management, &
Reliability through
Technology

FC

**FAST
COMPANY**
Press

Fast Company Press
New York, New York
www.fastcompanypress.com

This work is being published under the Fast Company Press imprint by an exclusive arrangement with Fast Company. Fast Company and the Fast Company logo are registered trademarks of Mansueto Ventures, LLC. The Fast Company Press logo is a wholly owned trademark of Mansueto Ventures, LLC.

Distributed by River Grove Books

Design and composition by Greenleaf Book Group and Teresa Muniz
Cover design by Greenleaf Book Group and Teresa Muniz
Previously published articles by Steven K. Richmond used with permission by Forbes and Machinery and Equipment MRO.

Publisher's Cataloging-in-Publication data is available.

Paperback ISBN: 978-1-63908-037-3

Hardback ISBN: 978-1-63908-038-0

eBook ISBN: 978-1-63908-039-7

First Edition

I've been blessed to work with so many smart people throughout my life, whether they have been mentors, coworkers, employees, friends, coaches, or family—and each has helped impact and define me. I want to dedicate this book to the communities of people that I have had incredible experiences and built amazing connections with. I am forever grateful to you all for shaping me into the person I am today.

AUTHOR'S NOTE

JOHN WOODEN WASN'T a good basketball coach. He was—and is—a legend. John Wooden won ten Division 1 basketball titles in twelve years, including seven in a row. In the early seventies, he had back-to-back undefeated teams, and as a player, he was the first to be named All-American three times. Coach Wooden was also the first person to be inducted into the Hall of Fame as both a player and a coach.

Basketball did not define John Wooden despite his success. Coach Wooden was humble, religious, and deeply committed to always doing the right thing. He was a great motivational speaker, and I had the pleasure of hearing him speak at a coaches' clinic early on a Sunday morning in Cincinnati, Ohio. He began the clinic with a prayer and followed it up with an apology for working on a Sunday, which he didn't believe in doing. He then explained that his employer, UCLA, had recently signed an agreement with a shoe company, and as part of that agreement, he was required to present at certain coaching clinics. Despite his feelings about working on Sunday, he felt his obligation was to fulfill the agreement of his employer.

I have enjoyed reading about Coach Wooden ever since, and he has left behind a plethora of wisdom. Some of which you will see from time to time in this book.

CONTENTS

Introduction 1

⚙ **Chapter 1** Designing with the End in Mind................ 11

⚙ **Chapter 2** Prioritize What Is Truly Critical.................. 29

⚙ **Chapter 3** It's All about Process.................................... 49

⚙ **Chapter 4** Consistency Is Key...................................... 57

⚙ **Chapter 5** Reactions to Change.................................... 65

⚙ **Chapter 6** Prepare for the Unexpected 79

⚙ **Chapter 7** People.. 93

⚙ **Chapter 8** Staying Safe and Smart.............................. 107

⚙ **Chapter 9** What's on the Horizon 119

Appendix Select Articles by Steve K. Richmond 131

Additional Resources 149

Notes 151

About the Author 155

INTRODUCTION

*"Whatever you do in life, surround yourself with
smart people who'll argue with you."*

—John Wooden

THE MAINTENANCE AND reliability industry can be worth hundreds of billions of dollars if we embrace the way technology gives us valuable information. One of the key concerns of any enterprise is reliability. Whether you are making automobiles or crackers, running a hospital or a customer service center, recycling scrap metal or figuring out how to occupy Mars, reliability is key. And today, technology is a critical component of any reliability solution.

For over three decades, I've helped companies across a variety of industries put technology to work in their maintenance and reliability efforts. There is a human factor to technology-enabled reliability, and regardless of the type of business or the company's goal, I've seen what approaches work well. Even as technology changes, managing the human side of reliability stays consistent.

> Even as technology changes, managing the
> human side of reliability stays consistent.

Technology changes at a fast and furious pace. But the best strategies for using technology to get the most out of a business's assets are tried and true. In this book, I'll give you some insights on how anyone in the maintenance and reliability industry, regardless of the size of your organization or the product or service you are connected to, can leverage technology to make the most of what you have today and tomorrow, whatever the future brings.

WORKING HARD AND SMART—IT'S IN MY DNA

I grew up on the west side of Cincinnati. My father was a "Proctoid"— Cincinnati's affectionate term for employees of Proctor & Gamble, headquartered here in town. After he got out of the Marine Corps, my dad's first job was to load boxes of Ivory Soap into boxcars. He went to night school, got a degree in industrial engineering, and worked his way up within the company.

I've always followed my dad's example of hard work and determination. When I was a teenager in the late 1960s, he encouraged me to take my first real job at a company doing residential heating, ventilation, and air-conditioning (HVAC). He believed the best problem solvers were tradespeople, and that it was best to launch into the working world with a trade skill under your belt. So I learned to thread pipe, hang sheet metal ductwork, and install complete systems by the age of sixteen.

As much as I liked working with my hands, I began to gravitate toward management. After graduating college, I took a job managing a crew for a company that owned large tracts of real estate. We kept HVAC systems and appliances operational for thousands of apartments all over the metropolitan area. By the mid-1980s, I had over forty vehicles running around the city ensuring that thousands of pieces of mechanical equipment were well maintained—all tracked on paper by hand.

Our company lived with two main concerns: scheduling preventative maintenance on all that equipment and providing speedy responses to emergency equipment failures.

I knew technology might address the uncertainty inherent in our system, so I bought an Epson PC with dual 5¼" floppy drives and some software. I put what I was doing on paper into the software system and began to make sense of some of the chaos.

INFORMATION IS THE MOST VALUABLE ASSET

Around the end of the 1980s, it occurred to me that the information around maintenance and reliability was ultimately more valuable than the actual work itself. Armed with technical knowledge and a budding interest in software solutions to these kinds of operations, I launched my company Projetech in 1990 and began managing technical projects for my clients.

Soon it became clear that my clients, always in search of better reliability and less downtime, needed better information. They needed something computerized to track all aspects of their equipment (life cycles, parts, costs, vendors, etc.). If a machine went down, by having all the information about that machine, they could determine what maintenance was required to ensure long-term reliability, what additional work would be cost-effective, and how quickly they would be able to go back online. Since no one can predict when a machine is going to break down, they needed to have all the information about all aspects of the machine on hand and constantly up-to-date. In short, they needed a computerized maintenance management system. Projetech began helping clients purchase, install, and configure these systems and training clients' staff on how to use them.

Larger software companies saw the potential of maintenance management systems. In the mid-1990s, Project Software & Development, Inc, developed a software product called Maximo®, a system that manages the physical assets of a business throughout each asset's lifetime. Within a few years, Maximo became the system of choice for our clients because of its ability to track and manage asset data through the life cycle; planned and unplanned work activities; service offerings, agreements, and delivery; contracts; inventory; and procurement.

THE PARALLEL EVOLUTION OF COMMUNICATIONS AND TECHNOLOGY

The evolution of technology has run parallel in a pretty straight line with that of bandwidth or communications technology. It's like Marshall McLuhan said: "The medium is the message." When he first said that in the 1960s, he was referring to whether someone was listening to the radio or the spoken word or reading and how that choice of medium impacted what was being conveyed. I have seen the same with our ability to communicate and the technology available to us.

Consider the simple phone call. Way back in the day, we had party lines and had to wait our turn to use the telephone and then hope no one was eavesdropping on our conversation. Then we moved to each household having their own phone line, but we had to be thoughtful about when to use long distance. Remember waiting to talk to Grandma in California until after 8:00 p.m. on Friday because the rates were cheaper? Now we can join our colleagues on a multiperson video call from literally anywhere in the world anytime we want for a very reasonable flat subscription rate. We all talk to one another more today than decades before because it is easy and cheap to do so.

The internet went through the same type of evolution. The U.S. Advanced Research Projects Agency Network, better known as ARPANET, was the beginning of what we call the internet today. AOL brought it to the masses by mailing you a CD, and, even before that, a floppy disk. You would load software onto your computer, buy a modem, and beat your head against the wall for a few hours trying to make your dial-up connection work before you finally got your friend to come over and help you figure out how to get online. And then once you got online, what could you do? The internet then was basically text-based, with a lot of message boards and some basic websites.

All of that evolved. Soon, we started to see computer systems that were singular machines typically built with processes designed to accomplish a specific, individual goal. Most effective early PC software programs were accounting-based—the problems the software was asked to deal with were black-and-white and didn't require a lot of interpretation. And when companies first brought PCs to their small- to medium-sized businesses, they did so for those accounting products. The early PCs were very expensive, clunky, and isolated.

But then people began to be able to connect these devices with coaxial cable, thus creating rudimentary networks. Those very early forays into the connectivity of these machines allowed them to branch out to other uses beyond accounting. So, if the marketing team had a word processing product and they were working on copy for the next press release or advertisement, suddenly the marketing people and the finance people had the ability to share information in some ways. After that, product development and engineering and other departments would see reasons to connect. Eventually the entire company would be connected in a basic, limited but functional, local area network. Connectivity between geographies was pretty much limited to contiguous office space and didn't take off until the late 1980s, when we started seeing a more dial-up DSL followed by the original 56K modem.

Those evolutions of being able to communicate with more people faster and for machines to exchange information all evolved around telecommunications improvement. This lit a fire under management to understand what developments were going on in the software and technology worlds and what could be done with them. These standalone systems, perhaps doing some rudimentary tracking of mechanical systems maintenance, were similar to the way I first started using software to schedule my maintenance crew instead of using a whiteboard or index cards.

Those types of systems evolved very quickly because smart people kept improving them and sharing them. Soon people realized that there was something that might be of value to somebody else and started selling early maintenance management software. The idea took off, and that type of software soon was available in the hundreds.

Anybody with a PC and a garage could write product code back then. In fact, a book I bought around 1990 was devoted to listing the ninety-three maintenance management software products available at the time, comparing capabilities, pricing, and so on. As with all young industries, so many of those products didn't survive, but a few good ones did.

Communication capabilities continued to increase. We evolved from text-based to graphics-based software, and speed improved as latency—the interruption of packets of information moving across a computer line causing the dreaded "blue screen of death"—went down. This allowed the capabilities of maintenance management software to grow, and the evolution continued. Today we have wireless technology. The processing power we have with the phones in our pockets is greater than what was used to send a man to the moon sixty years ago.

And that's the space I lived in that interested me—watching that evolution, that constant change, and the leaps in capability that came with it. Not just for the sake of fancier technology, but also because it meant learning more from everything we were doing with maintenance and reliability so we could keep saving time and money.

Now we have artificial intelligence (AI), in which a machine can take the information provided and react to it with a command almost instantaneously. It's an extremely powerful concept, but it's enabled by the communication evolution to almost limitless bandwidth and ultrafast connectivity.

Several new cars today have features that enable your automobile to see something on the road ahead and react to it much quicker than you can. That's because the processing speed and the communication capabilities are there. This will be extrapolated into a wider band of information when fully automated driving comes to be as cars talk to one another and to their main systems at even greater speeds of information exchange. Then the car will react not only to what the individual driver or car may see or know but also to what the cars ahead of it are seeing and reacting to, and what the central system says is happening on this particular tract of road on a daily basis at 5:00 p.m. All that information is instantaneously available, and it's all communications-driven. Now we're starting to make decisions from an artificial perspective, faster and better than we humans can. And while in maintenance, you still need a guy with a wrench to make certain repairs and judgments about what needs to be done, the machines themselves are going to be making more and more of these decisions better and faster than we could have ever imagined—all thanks to the evolution of communications.

FASTER, BETTER MAINTENANCE DECISIONS

Our capability to manage assets and improve maintenance and reliability continues forward with expansion of communications and technology. We're seeing new and better ways to react fast or make decisions that take maintenance and reliability to a new level. But as we build better systems, it's critical to not only have the right information at the start but also then study very carefully how this information interacts and make sure that the right information is being exchanged at the right time in an efficient process so that we get the results we're after.

The old adage of "garbage in, garbage out" remains applicable today. We need to be careful that we're entering the correct information in the right format. We must look at where this information needs to go and who it needs to be shared with, what systems need to be able to touch it, what systems might benefit from it, and what systems can add value to it. Going forward, most network technology going forward will be software-defined. The flow charts we've made for years will soon be created by artificial intelligence (AI), based on the inputs our systems provide. Artificial intelligence, especially as the software starts to become corrective in nature, will correct even some of our subtle mistakes and make what we started with better by offering us suggestions for improvement. But those recommendations only have value if they're based on good data in the system that reflect what we wanted to accomplish when we started down this path of improving maintenance and reliability.

START SMART, CONTINUE STRONG

I believe that even though change from the evolution of technology and communications is happening faster and more effectively, there are some basic tenets to keep in mind as you build or improve a maintenance management system. First off, the maintenance and reliability industry is a multibillion-dollar business, and sometimes we can get bogged down in the immensity of what it is we're trying to accomplish. I've always been a fan of grabbing the low-hanging fruit, starting with what you can control early and building upon that, step-by-step, brick-by-brick. Begin first with what you know best—the data that you know is solid with a sound history behind it. Use that as the baseline for what it is you're trying to build and then expand it out from there. It will get to critical mass over time. But trying to tackle the whole at the outset, in my view, is inefficient and, unless you have unlimited money and time, very difficult to do well.

People are an integral part of the entire process. It's important to get them on board and document their collective experience. It's wise to heed the warnings about "the rusting of the American brain." Don't let your seasoned employees retire and take a tremendous amount of knowledge with them as they walk out the door. Try to capture that wisdom in some fashion as best you can before they leave and transform it into a knowledge base to leverage going forward.

There's no question that people are critical, but equally crucial are good processes because, at its heart, maintenance and reliability is a process business. I believe that software will help us with better process development, but only if we can sketch out how our process functions. You need to have a documented way to do things that's repeatable and that everybody understands and follows. If you can't tell me how it works, and if it doesn't make sense or function well today, better technology and communications won't help you; they will just generate bad information faster.

Do you need the fastest computer and a 10-gig fiber connection in the beginning? Absolutely not. Computers are inexpensive today compared to what they used to cost, so you can start with affordable equipment. You don't need expensive technology or the fastest connections to get started. All of that can grow as the need develops. As your system matures and grows, you can spend more on technology if it's necessary, or you can increase your bandwidth if that's what you need.

People, *process*, and *technology*—those are the fundamentals. All three are critical to good maintenance and reliability and to creating successful maintenance management systems.

As much as things change, they still remain the same. I think there's comfort in that adage. It means you can take future change in stride. I've always enjoyed studying history and learning from what other people have done because learning what has happened is a prescient window into what's to come. Whether the lessons from the past highlight mistakes or successes, understanding what worked and what didn't will be applicable to doing well going forward.

In this book, I highlight which strategies consistently help companies harness technology to make the most of their assets. I look at how companies approach change, how to efficiently employ or upgrade technology-driven processes, and how to get good data. I cover the people side of processes and staying secure, and I give you a peek at developments I see on the horizon. Overall, I hope I inspire you to follow one of the goals I've always set for myself, and that's to never stop learning. I'm never finished. But I do try to start smart and continue strong, and I hope what I have to share helps you do the same.

CHAPTER 1

DESIGNING WITH THE END IN MIND

*"Things work out best for those who make
the best of the way things work out."*

—John Wooden

YOU NEED TO know what you want to get out of a system before you create it. Otherwise, you run the risk of investing a lot of time and money in a system that doesn't give you the information you need or that falls short of delivering everything it is capable of. Or, conversely, it gives you so much information that the output isn't worth the effort you expended to get it.

I also think there need to be reasonable expectations when designing a system. The goals you set for systems need to match the organization's capabilities and infrastructure; otherwise you risk setting up your people for failure. It's important to be inclusive, inquisitive, and realistic from the beginning.

> It's important to be inclusive, inquisitive,
> and realistic from the beginning.

SEEK VALUE, NOT THINGS

Designing with the end in mind can start with the type of system that works best for your organization. Should it be on-site? Should it be run as a cloud-based service? Should it be a stand-alone system or incorporated into a comprehensive system?

It's easy to get bogged down in the details of these questions without first identifying what your organization truly needs. Especially when comparing the costs of different options, it's important to break down what is involved as far as capital and operating costs, expertise, and infrastructure for each alternative and make sure you're getting the value of what you want from what you are paying for. Sometimes the answer leads you to purchasing a service rather than building your own system.

Each day, I want to put on a fresh, clean shirt. For the sake of argument, let's think of the clean shirt as the maintenance and reliability needs of your company. Consider what it takes to invest in that clean shirt. I go to the supermarket and buy some Tide laundry detergent (for our argument, Tide is a software system). While I'm hoping to have a clean shirt each morning, all I did was buy Tide. I don't have a clean shirt yet. In order to clean that shirt on my premises, I'll also need the infrastructure and peripheral support.

I think most people don't want to buy software; they don't necessarily want Maximo, SAP ERP, or Oracle EAM. They don't need IBM WebSphere. They don't need MS operating systems or HP servers. They don't want to worry about intrusion equipment or virus protection. They just want a clean shirt—they just want their maintenance and reliability to work! In exchange for all the infrastructure that's needed to support the laundry detergent on premise, I could opt for a laundry service. Every morning I'd wake up, open my closet, and there on my hanger would be a clean shirt, ironed, packaged, finished. In the same way, software as a service (SaaS) is maintenance and reliability without all the extra *stuff*.

What You Need to Get a Clean Shirt	What You Need for an On-Premise Asset Management System
Laundry room	A datacenter
Washer and dryer	Servers
Heating/air-conditioning	Environmental control
110v and 220v electrical power supply	Adequate electrical power and data lines
Locks on the door	Security protection
Floor drain	Disaster recovery planning
Stain remover, fabric softener	Software add-ons for the maintenance management system

Software as a service, like a laundry service, can add tremendous value over the long-term. Over the years, I'll wash my shirt numerous times, and I'll have to keep buying more Tide and other consumables (i.e., servers will wear out and will need replacing). In fact, if I wash my shirt enough times, it will wear out too. The beauty of software as a service is that I'm always going to have a new shirt in my closet that fits because the service includes product upgrades and ongoing improvements. I can't get that with Tide by itself, and you don't get that with software on its own. On the other hand, by subscribing to software as a service, you get the software system, infrastructure, support, and security all in one. It's a great solution for small- to medium-sized businesses that need a system but don't have the investment capital needed for an on-premise system.

Most companies are familiar with software as a service and know that technologically it works. But not everyone stops to think through all the costs of building and maintaining their own system when comparing costs between operating systems in-house versus as a software service. Many say, "Oh, we can do this ourselves . . . I already own a washing machine, so it's free." No, it's not. It's important to lay out the cost of all the underlying things that go into the care and feeding of a product to be able to compare that cost accurately to the cost of a software service.

When comparing options, remember to include more than one side of the business, and be aware of needs for future expansion. Software as a service gives you some flexibility and some agility. You've got to make this capital and operational expense. And once you do, the areas of the business the system can serve really is limitless. You spend the first 80 percent to get it up and running. It doesn't cost you another 80 percent to involve operational people or production people, or even sales and marketing people. Those incremental departmental adds are smaller in terms of investment because the largest part of it has been taken care of. Once you have the service, the energy, ability, and capability to expand it and pivot into other areas are so much more practical than they would be if it were simply a product.

KNOW WHAT YOU WANT BEFORE YOU START

You're considering a maintenance management system because someone has convinced you it's going to provide you with something. What is that something? People spend huge sums of money to roll out a system because they want to solve a problem, but for some reason during the setup, they fail to communicate the original problem they wanted to solve.

For example, a widget producer installed a system. A few months down the road, someone logs on and decides she wants to do a search for how many blue widgets she has, but she can't answer the question. No one ever told the implementation team that they needed to track *blue* widgets. They only said, "We make a thousand widgets per day. We want to track them." Unfortunately, widget color differentiation was not part of the conversation. I can't give you a count on *blue* widgets if we're not tracking *blue* widgets. You have to begin (design system tracking) with the end (reporting needs) in mind.

When you install a system, you introduce your company to a major boost in its potential for data collection and reporting. You might be tempted to recycle the old reports from your previous system and continue doing what you've been doing all along. But to make the most of the reporting power of a system, it takes a little imagination up front to consider what you could do with that power. Let's say you've bought the product, fully installed the system, and trained the end users. You've developed the application and created all the reports, the project is finished, and it's a huge success. The question I like to ask is, What does it look like? Tell me what the world looks like in that euphoric state of "Damn! I wish I had done this five years ago!" Write it down; write down everything. What do you want this picture to be six months from now? What reports could you develop that would make your life easier?

Sometimes this is harder to do than you'd think. Some people don't know what they don't know, because they've never had a system that would give them this level of granularity in their dataset. That's when some outside help may be useful to help you think through what else you might want to track about your organization's processes.

Let's go beyond widgets and look at all the potential information waiting to be discovered in a relatively simple manufacturing operation: stamping steel oil pans. What questions can we ask? Likely, the team will be asked to track how many oil pans they are making in a given period of time, whether it's by the hour, day, or shift. That may lead to the question about how many good oil pans they are making. Maybe they're stamping out one thousand of them each day, but they have two hundred defective pans that leak. Their real output is eight hundred. So, there's the metric of how many they're making and the metric of how many defective ones they have to throw away; that gives us a net output. How does that reflect the amount of money and time we spend on maintenance?

WHAT ABOUT SCRAP?

And there is another area, called scrap, that is tracked in a business like this. How much scrap are we creating? We're taking a sheet of metal, sticking it into a hydraulic press, and trying to make an oil pan out of it. Well, sometimes that process fails immediately, and it doesn't even get to be a defective oil pan. It's just a ruined piece of steel because something went wrong. So what's our scrap content? What's our scrap output? How many pounds of scrap are we making? The time and money we're spending to make that hydraulic press more reliable or work better—in general to do a better job—is a measurable output of increase.

The press uses a lot of cutting oil. If you have leaks or a press that's not working optimally, you could have high oil usage or high lubricant usage. Now you're starting to talk about costs. What does it cost to make the oil pan? We've got the raw cost of the steel, but you have to factor in the high cost of lubricants because the machine isn't operating correctly.

And what about safety? How many accidents per one thousand hours are we reporting or recording? And how safely is the process being operated for everybody involved?

Then there's transportation safety—getting the raw material to the machine. It's heavy, bulky, awkward stuff that's dangerous to put in place. Once it's in place in the operation, there is the safety of moving individual sheets into a punch press. Almost all of this is done robotically today, but if it's done by hand, keeping hands clear of the punch press is still important.

And that leads to personal protective equipment (PPE). Face shields, gloves, big leather aprons (oftentimes worn by the operators), steel-toed shoes, hearing protection. How much PPE are we using? If that rate changes, what does that tell us?

Then again, there's the transportation of that finished product and how safely it's packaged and shipped. There's testing that has to go on, typically to make sure that the oil pan holds up to pressure. That leads to the safety of the testing stations themselves and the compressed air used during the testing to apply pressure to the pans.

Of course, any scrap is inherently dangerous, with a lot of sharp edges, and it is hard to handle because it's bulky. The transportation of the scrap bin to a larger bin at the exterior of the facility and then transporting it off-site becomes another safety point to measure.

That's probably not an exhaustive list of things that the oil pan stamping company could be tracking, nor will the company choose to track everything on their list. But by asking questions, they can decide what they want to know.

Define what you want to know. Then, work backward from that result set and break it down: Where does each result come from? What are the components of it? Those are the things that need to be prioritized, documented, and managed. Those are the things that give us the outcomes we're looking for.

AVOID SILOS

So now we know the value in asking questions to find out what information is important to track. But which questions? That probably depends on *who* you ask.

Often, we begin our work with one business unit within a company. That department has a need; there is something about their business unit that they're trying to solve. Many times, I see very similar opportunities in parallel departments within the same organization. It's important to include more than one area of the business when building a system in order to get the full picture of what the data can do.

Let's look back at our example of the company that stamps steel oil pans. Would all those questions come from the same department? Likely not. Operations would ask about production numbers, defects, and scrap. Maintenance would ask about detecting leaks from the quantity of cutting oil being used. Health and safety would ask about accidents and PPE. All of this information comes together to give a picture about the total cost of producing oil pans. But if only one department was involved in the design of the system, parts of the picture would be missing. We've tracked maintenance time and material, but can we match that up with the planned production goals? Are we making more oil pans today because our equipment is more reliable? Are our costs going down because our safety record is better or because we're making fewer parts? We need to track everything needed to answer these questions.

The maintenance and the operations group are typically separate organizations, and they tend to run somewhat autonomously. But everybody—quality production, operations, maintenance, human resources, health and safety, and others—needs to be in the room when you start talking about this. Everyone's needs are different, and it's good for people to understand what everybody else's needs are. If I ask someone to do something sixty days from now that doesn't seem to them to be important, I have to understand and be able to explain to that person why it's really important to another department.

Let's look at another example in which I've seen lost opportunity from a silo approach, and that's hospitals. Often the team that oversees the hospital building envelope will want to install a system. They will have concerns about air-conditioning equipment, doors, light bulbs, doorknobs, and so on. Maybe they'd also track hospital beds or backup generators or things like that. But another group down the hall is working with high-touch patient equipment, machinery for dialysis, and heart monitors, all of which could benefit from tracking important information. In fact, if I were looking at the hospital as a whole, the biomedical equipment would be the first item I would include. But the biomedical people rarely connect with the maintenance people. It's like expecting to find the hockey team intermingling with the bowling team—it doesn't happen very often.

I've seen the same thing happen with airports. The facilities department asks for a system, and we track HVAC and other equipment related to the building envelope. But we find out there are millions of dollars' worth of assets classified as ground service equipment: the fuel tankers, the tugs that push the planes, all the equipment and machinery that goes into getting the bags from the front of the airport into the planes. But because we're only working with the facilities team, the most expensive assets are overlooked.

Of course, there is a lot of value to any group using systems for their specific needs. But there's a bigger opportunity there, and it may take a senior executive to authorize incorporating all the departments needed to include the company's most valuable and informative assets. If done well, all the company's systems can come together in a network operations center (NOC). One system can house data from field operations, production, facilities, engineering, safety, and so on. And you can start to look at a complete picture as opposed to bits and pieces of it.

What you gain is efficiency and accuracy. Let's say you're dealing with a power disruption. With the information you have in the NOC, you can see that an alarm is signaling that a turbine that should be making electricity is down. You can quickly access your grid and reallocate power. You have the maintenance schedule for the power lines at your fingertips and know who is working closest to the down turbine and coordinate the needed labor. You can pull up the engineering drawings of the turbine and that section of the grid quickly for the maintenance crew. With a consolidated system, you have more data you can work with.

From 2020 to 2022, we saw a whole new level of value from consolidated systems when people around the world had to work remotely during the COVID-19 pandemic. Those companies whose systems allowed them to share information across functions likely had a more efficient transition. And those that had been reluctant to digitize their systems suddenly found digitization necessary.[1]

LESSONS FROM COVID-19, ZOOM, AND UBER

What fascinates me about what happened in the first two years of the COVID-19 pandemic is that the move to working remotely didn't require any new tools. The technology was always there, but the reason to use it changed. Zoom went to the stratosphere overnight, but Zoom technology had already been there for years.

Ten years ago, I put cameras and big monitors in my conference room.

At that time, it was a hefty monetary investment to do so, and I tried to get my employees to spend more time on video calls. I don't know why they resisted it. I would walk into a meeting room and say, "Hey, why don't we have this on the camera?" I could feel their eyes rolling back in their heads. But with the pandemic, it became a necessity.

Not all employers embraced the idea before the pandemic, either. For many, remote work was taboo. Some people didn't believe in it at all. And yet there were smaller examples of successes with remote work that should have let people know that it was a practical alternative. For example, some small- to medium-sized companies for years would allow maternity leave extensions as long as employees stayed in touch and were accessible from time to time, or there were predefined hours blocked when the employee was available to communicate. Or if someone had an extended injury or illness—an office worker was very sick or had a broken hip, for example—and could still contribute to their jobs but just couldn't physically move about, they were allowed to work remotely. But it wasn't celebrated as a success. Nobody wanted to admit it worked as well as it did.

Today I'm seeing advertisements by a venture capital group raising money to build residential enclaves in Belize specifically for people who want to move there to work, because now people can work from anywhere.

Uber is another example of existing technology finally being put to use. Nothing Uber did was new or revolutionary. They took GPS and handheld equipment, the need for people to get from point A to point B, and the fact that some people wanted some part-time work to put cash in their pockets. They took a side hustle and a cell phone and GPS and put together a service that's changed transportation.

Sometimes it takes someone to have an epiphany to leverage technology that's always been there right under our collective noses. It also takes overcoming whatever fear of trying something new lies behind the barriers we put up. With remote work or using apps to schedule service, sometimes there is a fear of technology replacing human connection. And granted, some human connection, such as young children building relationships with their teachers and classmates, is harder over video conference than in person. But in other cases, it brings people together who weren't connecting before, such as families that live in different parts of the country getting in the habit of Zooming every month. But one thing I think we have learned from the pandemic is that we don't have to have a blanket fear of technology hurting human connection—we just have to find the right balance.

We also have to keep an eye on the bottom-up bubble that happens with technology, such as young people texting one another since they were nine years old. Now they're thirty and part of our workforce. For them, communicating quickly and effectively with something in their hand is what they've always done. During the pandemic, we had both forces at work: the bottom-up push of we're connected anyway on our personal devices and the tearing down of the resistance from above because using technology to work remotely was the only way to stay in business. The two forces came together, and technology once resisted was now accepted. We saw that reflected in Zoom's stock price during the first nine months or so of the pandemic.

We can learn from Uber and Zoom and the pandemic. The next time a technology solution is presented to you that's new in your maintenance reliability sphere and you are concerned that it will replace or hamper the human connection, step back and think about that. Will it really? Instead of saying no right off the bat, see if there is a way to test it and tweak it to make it work. We do have to have the human side of our work. We can't let any technology take away the human feel, but we need to test it to see if that problem will actually come to pass, because we may be surprised.

STOP "BACKING INTO MAINTENANCE"

How many kids do you know who ride around on their bicycles with little license plates on the back that say "Maintenance Engineer"? Personally, I don't know of any. The kids I know who want to be engineers want to be *electrical* engineers, *mechanical* engineers, or *chemical* engineers. Everyone wants to do the engineering work, but no one wants to do the maintenance. The maintenance crew spends all their time in the basement, hanging out in the boiler room or manning tool cribs. It's hot down there.

Often maintenance is seen as a necessary evil, but I've got news for you. If you go to LinkedIn and you look up the head of maintenance for XYZ Corporation, you're going to find electrical engineers, mechanical engineers, or chemical engineers. They didn't go to university to be a maintenance engineer.

I think a good number of U.S. businesses suffer from this same problem of backing into maintenance and reliability. We'll hire some big engineering company out of Chicago to design a power plant. We'll spend twelve years building it with the best and the brightest people MIT spits out, installing a turbine that will outclass anything in the world. After the ribbon cutting, the engineers move on, and the plant manager is supposed to take care of the facility. He's got plans and diagrams; he knows what materials it's made from. But the nitty-gritty of the maintenance plan tends to be an afterthought rather than something that is incorporated from the beginning.

Let's look at another example. We'll call this company Ainsworth's HVAC. Ainsworth's been in business for a few decades. Ainsworth started small, but he's grown steadily and now has approximately two hundred employees and eighty trucks on the road doing service calls. And Ainsworth ran into exactly this kind of trouble.

Ainsworth's has provided HVAC service for the oil pan company for years. They have a large boiler that fuels the hydraulic press that makes the oil pans. The boiler burns natural gas, heating water to the point of boiling to make steam. As is the case anytime you're injecting water into any process, over time the water calcifies and leaves behind residue. Eventually, the interior of that boiler needs to be cleaned. You need to be able to open up and get at those tubes and clean them from time to time. Occasionally one of them will rupture; it needs to be repaired or replaced.

This particular manufacturing plant was a single-story building built on a concrete slab. Very early on in the construction of the building, they set the boiler and started running pipes out to the areas of the plant where they needed the steam. And later on, the construction company came in and, in an effort to optimize plant floor space where manufacturing could take place, poured concrete and built a room around the boiler. It was just a matter of the footprint. Obviously, the guys pouring concrete and putting up walls weren't HVAC people.

Ainsworth's now can't open the faceplate on the boiler because the twenty-inch faceplate is eighteen inches from the wall. So what should have been a relatively straightforward servicing of the boiler becomes a bit of a construction project, because now they have to tear down a wall simply to be able to open the boiler and service it. A one- or two-day retube of a boiler turns into a few weeks of work. This is in addition to having to do demolition, the cost of the construction, and the line being down for that long.

If the company had thought to begin with the end in mind, they'd have asked questions like "How are we going to service this asset? Is there a design flaw with it? Should we use a different motor here in California than we use in Wichita?" When it comes to maintenance, many companies find that hindsight is 20/20. If you want to get your foresight a little closer to 20/20, the answer is to begin with the end in mind.

For many companies, their competitive advantage begins with the widget they produce. Over time, their widget becomes a commodity, and competition increases. Now it's the company's ability to be failure-free that makes them competitive in that market. By building a maintenance database on their equipment from the beginning, they would have gained a leg up in their long-term ability to remain competitive. If you want to drive failure out of the system, you need to improve quality, which is typically a function of reliability. They started building widgets and ended up maintaining the widget-making equipment. Many companies don't plan to do it this way. If you find yourself in a maintenance quandary down the road with no historical data, you could lose your competitive edge. Beginning with the end in mind from a reliability standpoint means that you start with maintenance and reliability best practices, rather than taking this into consideration when it's too late. By tracking failure, you can build toward efficiency and safety.

Recently I had a customer in the energy sector, specifically oil and gas, who was interested in growing their foothold in the industry. At the time, this company came to me asking about systems because they had recently purchased an offshore pipeline in Louisiana that was connected to a set of oil platforms in the Gulf of Mexico. They agreed on the product and the price, and the deal was done. When it came down to the transfer of assets, they didn't really know what they were getting. They decided to implement systems to capture all the data on the assets they had just acquired. They might know on paper that they have x sets of piping of this type, and y pumps of that type, and so on, but they hadn't captured it in a software system that would allow them to know how to preventatively maintain it. They understood that if they didn't do the preventative maintenance, then they would be painting themselves into a corner with a possible rip-and-replace if there was a failure later on. Obviously, this would be extremely expensive, so they planned to take the maintenance data that was on file with the acquired company and import it into a system. Going forward, this would allow them to set up preventative and corrective maintenance schedules based on the maintenance history. This is a case of "I don't know exactly what I just bought, and I've got to get it into a system so that I can manage it." It's one of the smartest examples of beginning with the end in mind. All that historic data on the acquired pipeline assets would be transferred to the system, creating an archive of downtime, maintenance, costs, and more, which will give the company easy access to reporting and trending right off the bat.

A CALIFORNIA STORY

We've had some great opportunities for learning over the years. This case study is a good one to illustrate how we needed to make changes in order to achieve results.

A water agency in Northern California offers many different services across two counties, including water supply, wastewater collection and treatment, management of ninety-two million gallons of water per day, and more.

Since 1996, the agency has been using Maximo to manage and maintain many assets from pumping plants and supplemental wells to pipelines, booster stations, and heavy equipment. Overall, the company was struggling with the lack of implementation standards, staff training and efficiency, the retirement of key IT personnel, and the absence of an IT manager with Maximo expertise. While the organization started with an in-house Maximo solution, it had to switch to a hosted environment and ended up with a Projetech cloud solution instead.

Maximo as a Service (MaaS) helped the business save time and cut IT expenditures without having to worry about implementation. MaaS provided enhanced availability of assets through any internet-connected device, and Maximo's robust, military-grade cloud security with key security certifications reassured the company that its data was safe and managed appropriately. California businesses are no stranger to natural disasters. Luckily, having MaaS's disaster recovery capability ensures that an organization's data is replicated in multiple U.S. locations and secure no matter what happens, so they can rest assured knowing they will not have issues in any event. Projetech and its industry partner dedicate themselves and Maximo experts to support the agency and help them succeed in maximizing the return on investment on Maximo.

By moving to the cloud, the organization achieved improved

continued

accessibility, enhanced security, and disaster recovery assistance. This is really significant as it services six hundred thousand people.

LOOK AHEAD AND LOOK BACK

We all like to build things to last, our computer systems included. Sometimes, it's worth engaging the design team in a what-if exercise to consider future needs you'll want the system to be able to contend with.

One example of not thinking about the what-ifs comes from a regional airline. They once got caught in a massive snowstorm and had to cancel flights. They had been using a crew-scheduling product that had been built in-house, and after forty-eight to seventy-two hours of not flying aircraft, they went back to work. When they tried to load their crew information into the system to disseminate what pilots were going to get what planes and where they were going to go, the entire system crashed.

The reason was that there never had been enough memory built into the system to handle an entire load from the get-go; it had always been a continuous process system. The airline started flying and had always flown, so net changes to the system day-to-day were a few hundred thousand lines of information. After they'd been shut down for a few days, they needed to load many millions of lines of information, which the system was never built to handle. This exacerbated the problem and extended that shutdown for many more days after the weather had cleared. It was simply the unintended consequences of a software product that wasn't thought through.

Anytime there's an unplanned circumstance, an accident, a shutdown, a large piece of equipment going offline, or an interruption of production, it's a golden opportunity to get everybody together and say, "Okay, what went wrong? What went right? If it were to happen again tomorrow morning at eight o'clock, what would we do differently?" Then it would be appropriate to go back through process and procedure training and make sure that, were such an event to happen a second time, you had a methodology for managing it and dealing with it.

A lot of companies build out process, technology, and procedures from a "this is where we are today; this is where we want to be tomorrow" perspective. They try to improve on the current state, but many of them don't take into account what a change from that current state might look like. In the event that the current state no longer exists, how will this change from the current to proposed state? How might that be affected by a fresh start, a new boot, as it were? In my business, we call that disaster recovery, and it not only consists of a written plan but also is a process that we execute on every so often to ensure that we can bring the system back from zero state to standard state over a period of time.

We do this in our business constantly. We are always asking, "What is the recovery point objective in the event of a failure?" There are thousands of companies out there that think they're safe. They do backups of their information, and everybody thinks that's a nice security blanket, but a very small percentage of those companies actually take a backup of their system, put it in a cleansed environment, and try to rebuild their system from nothing. They have all the data, they've got the tape or the digits, they've got the information, but if they ever tried to rebuild their system from that backup, do they know what is possible? Do they understand the procedure for doing it?

Consider not only weather problems but also cybersecurity concerns. Having a way to recover is critical. Even if you know you can't afford to do the full plan today, at least make sure everybody who has some responsibility there is aware of it so that when things change, they can jump on it.

Part of the postmortem is asking, "What could we do differently? What could we have done differently given the tools at our disposal today? What could we do differently in the future if we had wireless communication, if we had more people, if we had a disaster recovery team?" You might not be able to fund or afford these things now, but having a wish list will allow you to be able to handle future situations better. Involve the folks who know the systems well and ask them what technology is evolving quickly to help free up that blue sky brainstorming.

Dealing with in-house people is all well and good, but I believe that this is where professional organizations really bring value to the table. They write white papers, publish reports, and share information across hundreds of sites as opposed to just two or three.

Key Takeaways

- Know the value of what you want a system to provide before you begin the design process.

- Consider full business and future expansion when thinking through system design.

- Gather key potential users of the system from across all departments and brainstorm all the potential outputs you think you may want from the system.

- Get the authority you need to approve a consolidated system. More data results in greater efficiency and accuracy.

- Don't be afraid of new technology. Test it, tweak it, and see whether it can work for you.

- Good data helps you to consider maintenance and reliability on the front end.

- Use the powerful question "What if?" to help think through potential emergencies and how to prepare for and recover from them.

CHAPTER 2

PRIORITIZE WHAT IS TRULY CRITICAL

"Be quick, but don't hurry."

—John Wooden

ENTERPRISE ASSET MANAGEMENT systems are powerful. But trying to make them do everything possible for you can cost time and money. Companies need to determine what is truly critical, and there are many aspects to that question. Let's take a look at what is critical to consider with the system design, maintenance itself, and company processes.

STOP MAJORING IN THE MINORS

We've all seen it. A group knows they need to make a change. They know it is important. They want to get it right on the first try, so they study the problem from every angle and involve anyone who might have insight or be impacted. Then months go by, maybe even a year passes, and the team is still planning.

> **When designing, avoid paralysis by analysis.**

What happens in my experience is that, first and foremost, the team in charge of the change is too big. If you walk into your first meeting and see nine people at the table, you've got a problem; two or three people are all you need. And each of those nine people has an agenda. Some are trying to make sure that everybody understands that the project is their idea and they're going to get the credit for its success. Others are adamant about making sure that everybody knows they had nothing to do with this, so when it crashes and burns, it won't be their fault. And there's always a person or two who just likes to talk so everybody knows how smart they are.

What often happens to teams like this is that they end up "majoring in the minors," getting caught up in too many minor details. They're going to start by managing their assets, so the first thing they want to do is identify them. That seems like a good idea. But let's go back to our friend Ainsworth and his HVAC company and see how that could end up being time that could have been better spent.

The maintenance department of the research facility of Ainsworth's HVAC has been working to expand their contract with Ainsworth's company. They want Ainsworth to maintain 1,200 pieces of equipment in their million-square-foot manufacturing facility outside of town. Ainsworth starts asking himself questions about those 1,200 pieces of equipment. What types of units are out there? How many of each type? The nameplate information for each unit is obviously invaluable. Ainsworth's HVAC doesn't have a lot of technology. They still do a lot of documentation by hand. What's the most efficient way for them to capture all of that information?

So, Ainsworth is ready to send an employee out with a clipboard to go from station to station and write down all the information from each nameplate: type of unit, identifying number, model number, serial number, and so on. But the research facility wants to be sure they have a method for assigning the identification number in a way that works for everyone on the team. They meet over and over again to analyze different naming schemes. Six months pass, and they're still trying to decide whether the unit code should start with letters that identify the unit type or numbers that indicate what floor of the building the unit is on. Finally, they're ready to send out Ainsworth's technician, and he spends three hundred hours at one hundred dollars an hour methodically writing down every piece of data he can glean from each one of those 1,200 units.

By now, so much time has gone by, and all those meetings and Ainsworth's employee's efforts have cost a lot of money in time. And the more time goes by, the more divisive people become over small details. At the end of the day, it's unlikely that the data on every single unit will be needed. This is a maintenance department; they only need the data when they need to fix a unit. A lot of time, money, and energy has been spent collecting more data than is needed.

I've always thought that it's best to let people continue to do their jobs. If the air conditioner breaks in building number one of the research facility, they call Ainsworth and his HVAC mechanic goes and finds out what the problem is. While he resolves the problem, he also jots down all the information about that piece of equipment. This way, he's collecting data on the machines that the company will actually spend time fixing.

TWO BIRDS, ONE STONE

Simply collect the data you need as you do the maintenance work. That way you're collecting just the information you need. Even if you have to go back here and there and update your information when you find you want to tweak how you track the data, the cost associated with making those changes is just a handful of hours, not the hundreds of hours spent collecting data that's never used.

It's easy to see how companies can go down this road. It's laudable that companies want to get to the root cause of whatever they are working on. That's often why they implement digital systems to manage their assets in the first place. But if the team gets too caught up in minutiae in order to make sure they've covered everything, they've gone too far.

A project has to have a sponsor—somebody in charge. As I've shared, one of my tenets is that you always should begin with the end in mind. I begin projects by asking, "What's the goal here? What are we trying to accomplish? Pick the three most important things that you want to get out of this effort today. You can have another list of day two initiatives that you want to do tomorrow. But on day one, what three things are we going to accomplish?" And then, in future meetings when the conversation deviates from the goal, I'll ask, "Does what we're talking about impact one of the three things we identified for day one? If not, then it's a day two conversation, and we'll talk about that when we attack day two."

Internal meetings should always have note takers, and there should be tasks assigned. And most importantly, there should be a date for completion. If you don't have a timeline, you don't have a target. Without a target, there is nothing to hit; you're never going to get anywhere. You need a line in the sand. And if one isn't there, make one.

LESSONS FROM Y2K

The greatest artificial line in the sand ever was Y2K. We worked with many companies that were operating old DOS-based systems with two-character years and had to convert those systems by December 1999. At first, there was no urgency—everyone involved had other work that was more pressing, and nothing was getting done. Then, when there were about 120 days left until the calendar flipped from 1999 to 2000, C-suite executives started to show up to meetings about Y2K preparedness. What was made abundantly clear to everyone was that Y2K was going to be a showstopper. Their old systems were not going to work after the first of the year, and that would impact their ability to pay for or receive materials or pay employees—basically it would affect their ability to operate. They now had a ninety-day window to make decisions and get them done. Suddenly, people became more likely to agree on a topic and move on to the next.

Often the smartest approach is to partner with someone who's already done this type of installation in the past and understands maintenance and reliability. Experience is always better, right? The best implementation team is one with experience who can give you the right advice to make sure that you're tracking the level of detail you need. They can talk you through your processes to be sure that you're capturing exactly the kind of data you need to capture.

IDENTIFYING CRITICAL ASSETS

You have to prioritize what you're trying to do. You could have a thousand assets, but only a subset of those assets are critical. You need to know what they are and most importantly, everyone in the organization needs to know what they are. They've got to be able to repeat it; it almost needs to be a mantra: What critical assets can't afford to be offline?

This was something the Japanese manufacturers I worked with were great at. For their assembly lines or production facilities, everything had a flow chart and the color of the asset on that chart would determine its criticality (i.e., if this thing doesn't work, nothing works). Toyota in Georgetown, Kentucky, made 272 Camrys, reliably hitting that target nearly every shift in 1985. They knew what things to concentrate on, and they did it the same way every time. That number may seem low today when companies like Tesla put out a car a minute. Toyota was best in class at the time, though, and a lot of people have emulated their approach over the years.

Prioritization, standardization, and tracking what you do—these are the keys to a strong system. The person who's there to troubleshoot or try to repair or improve something that might not be operating appropriately has got to trust that the tasks that have been listed prior to them were done in the right order and in the right way. If you standardize the way you do things and you've got good processes and procedures around prioritization, you've got a pretty good basis for a system.

With information systems, prioritization is just as critical as it is on an assembly line. The trick is not to get stuck trying to make the system perfect, or the cost of gathering data could outweigh the data's value.

Often, when a group first implements a system, the team wants to put every single piece of equipment into the system because they don't want to miss the ability to track something. But there's a cost to doing that. It's much more efficient to get the system up and running and then collect data on the critical assets as you go. If you have a hundred thousand assets, typically only twenty or twenty-five of them ever really require your attention on a regular basis. After two or three years of using a new system and gathering data as issues arise, you will have identified the devices that need your attention based on real need.

Let's check back in with Ainsworth and his HVAC company. Ainsworth had a contract with a large hospital. Part of his contract is to patrol the entire building twice a year to inspect each and every water fountain to check that the refrigeration is operating correctly and that the coils are clean or need to be vacuumed. Have you ever stopped to think about just how many water fountains there are in a hospital? When it comes to the inspection, there isn't much to do: Is it there? Check. Does it work? Check. There's nothing to it; if it breaks, you replace it.

After a year of this routine, Ainsworth decided to check in with the head of maintenance to see if this was really what made sense. Together they looked over maintenance data from the hospital's system. It showed that Ainsworth's crew spent 1,100 hours a year checking water fountains. At ninety dollars an hour, those walk-throughs cost the hospital $99,000 a year. The water fountains only cost $900 each to replace, considering both parts and labor, and the hospital kept two spares in stock. So far, the walk-throughs had only found one malfunctioning water fountain. Ainsworth and the head of maintenance agreed that it was too expensive to keep inspecting the water fountains. It cost less to just replace them should one break. By having data, Ainsworth's client made a cost-saving decision.

The scenario we painted with our friend Ainsworth happens often in real life. In a perfect world, the engineers who installed the equipment should hand you a comprehensive list of every nut, bolt, and screw as part of the final stage of installation. Unfortunately, this rarely happens. Typically, in large-scale operations in the energy sector, for instance, there are "walk down" crews. The walk down crew trolls the entire facility, collecting the same data that the engineers just carried out the door in their laptops. Walk down crews are there just to collect the same data all over again.

Asset-intensive organizations work hard to meet the challenge of balancing utilization loads across their asset portfolios. In an effort to keep equipment up and running, many organizations overstock assets and stock-pile parts in order to ensure fast repairs and continued operations. The problem they face is that all these additional equipment and parts also need to be kept in working order, which actually adds cost rather than ultimately reducing cost.[1] The act of trying to be reliable needs to provide return on investment (ROI), or there isn't any justification for it.

If you're inspecting water fountains, there's no ROI. On the other hand, if you're changing oil in a multimillion-dollar pump in a power plant, that's a different story. If you can demonstrate that changing the oil decreases the failure rate, and you know you will lose $35,000 per minute when the turbine goes offline, then you can determine mathematically what value your oil change provides. By employing an asset management software tool, organizations can be efficient about what spare parts they stock for backup while being smarter about the maintenance they perform on their asset portfolio. Efficient maintenance planning and a lower fixed capital investment can directly contribute to a better bottom line.[2]

CRITICALITY IN MAINTENANCE

Typically, we take for granted the reliability of the stuff around us. For example, we assume that the heating or air-conditioning in our home will be at the temperature we've set it to be. We want the house to be comfortable, so we set the thermostat to seventy-two degrees. On average, we don't think much about these systems until we come home from work on a sunny day and the internal temperature of the house is up to eighty-five degrees. Suddenly, there's a problem with the A/C, but only now do we ask ourselves, "Have we been diligent in changing the filter regularly? Is the condenser clean?" In general, people run these kinds of systems without a second thought until they break down. They rarely take maintenance into consideration, if at all.

In the early history of American industrialization, businesses tended to take a similar approach to maintenance. They would build a widget and use it until it broke. Maintenance was entirely a matter of responding to down equipment. When the equipment was broken beyond repair, someone might suggest that the next one could be built better than the last one, given that the last one broke in a certain way. Maintenance was an afterthought—the idea of *preventative* maintenance came relatively late in history. Equipment was first built to do a particular job, and the maintenance needed on the equipment was the product of inefficient thinking. Only after realizing the costs of failures and burdensome maintenance would the equipment redesign begin to factor in the maintenance life cycle.

This thinking led to the evolution of oil change frequency in our cars. In the early days of the internal combustion engine (ICE), automobile manufacturers recommended that drivers change their oil as frequently as every five hundred miles. Can you imagine doing that today? We'd be forced to change our oil every other week at that rate! As more people bought cars, more roads got paved, and then, of course, people drove their cars even farther and more frequently. With the introduction of inexpensive cars like Ford's Model T, more people could obtain cars. The cycle between oil changes was so short that more and more cars missed their scheduled oil change. It wasn't long before the increasing engine failure rate led manufacturers to respond.

Oil filters were introduced in the 1920s, and as time went on, constant improvements were made to oil pumps, filter design, and quality of oil. These upgrades enabled ICE cars to go three thousand miles between oil changes—while also extending the life of the engine to one hundred thousand miles or better—a maintenance standard that lasted for decades.

Today, technology once again challenges our thinking. Thanks to constant improvements in engineering, we're starting to change the oil in our cars even less frequently. The *New York Times* explored this idea a couple of years ago, noting that to determine the optimum oil change cycle, we need to make a relatively complicated calculation, factoring in the vehicle make, model, and age, along with the manufacturer's maintenance recommendations.[3] On top of the vehicle's mechanical data, we also need to consider the driver's driving type. A driver can have a "severe" driving type, meaning that they tend to make short trips in heavy city traffic, or the driver can have a "mild" driving type, meaning that they tend to put long highway miles on the car. This new approach to changing engine oil means that we can now go 7,500 or even 10,000 miles between oil changes. Obviously, the benefit is that we are able to better conserve petroleum resources and save time and money on maintenance. And even though the oil change is less frequent, we're actually optimizing our vehicle's life span.

The lesson is that you can no longer rely on your daddy's advice on car maintenance to best optimize ICE performance. Instead, we now need to make a complicated, informed calculation by tracking our use of the vehicle to determine the optimum maintenance cycle. Fortunately, we can get a little help in this calculation with on-board computing. Thanks to asset management software built into most cars today, the vehicle's computer is able to determine many of the variables in the equation, including the driver's driving type. The computer constantly monitors these variables and identifies when the next oil change is due.

The history of the automobile is a great one to consider because it has more than one hundred years of history behind it and has entered the twenty-first century having kept up with technology beautifully. Asset-intensive companies would do well to follow this example in their own maintenance programs. To improve ROI over the long term, these businesses need to have the ability to modernize and adapt with trends in technology, all while making use of computer systems that optimize maintenance and reliability for their existing asset portfolio.

FAILURE TEACHES CRITICALITY

One of my favorite professors in college gave a lecture I'll never forget. The topic was "pressure vessels." Essentially, a pressure vessel is a container that holds any gas or liquid under pressure. They were introduced during the advent of steam power more than 175 years ago, and they continue to be used in all kinds of applications today. The first reciprocating machines were steam-driven, before we started burning oil. Pressure vessels have been used on steam locomotives, steam-powered manufacturing equipment, and today can be found in applications ranging from gas storage tanks (oxygen or nitrogen tanks), anhydrous ammonia tanks, autoclaves, hot water storage tanks, chemical reactors, and refrigerant vessels.

My professor began his lecture by holding a four-inch-thick hardbound book above his head and slamming it down on his desk to wake us up. He patted the book and said, "This is the pressure vessel code book: It's 650 pages long; it contains 14,000 rules and regulations; and there isn't one passage in this book that didn't originate with someone's death." We build and design to prevent death ahead of time, building in safety, but most rules exist because someone got killed or injured in a mechanical failure. It might seem extreme, but the ultimate bottom line measure for reliability is whether or not someone died today.

For example, we now have rules regarding pressure vessels on the number of bolts needed on a joint, tank inspection, confined space entry, and other safety aspects of building, using, and maintaining these vessels.[4] Each rule and regulation reflects a lesson learned the hard way, but we'd like to learn these lessons before something goes wrong. Enter technology.

Computer modeling enables us to anticipate potential points of failure, which tends to result in safer products and technologies right out of the box. For example, for pressure vessels, a digital twin of the tank can be constructed through computer modeling and then simulations run to test pressure limits, reactions in different environments, circuitry configurations, and so on. Not only is it a safer way to test the design, it's also faster. A computer simulation can try a thousand different safety circuit configurations in a few minutes that would have taken days, weeks, or even months to test manually.

As technology advances, so do the ways we can improve safety while testing for safety. Drones are an excellent example and, equipped with cameras or sensing devices, are now used for inspections in a variety of industries. Korean Air has taken the use of drones a step further. Every time a plane lands, historically it's been a copilot's job to walk around and inspect a plane for loose parts or damage. Korean Air uses not just one hand-operated drone but also four preprogrammed drones to inspect a plane all at once. What used to take ten hours for the copilot to accomplish now takes the group of drones only four.[5]

INTRODUCING SPOT®

Boston Dynamics developed Spot*, a four-legged, nimble, battery-powered robot equipped with cameras. It looks like a cross between a grasshopper and a dog, but it can manage just about any terrain, weather, or air-quality conditions. The robot can get in and around areas and do things that would be injurious or impossible for us to do based on the safety of the environment. Consider the pressure vessels once again, and how dangerous it can be for a person to enter a confined space to clean a tank that is used to hold a gas or chemical. A robot like this one could do the work without putting a person in danger.

And Spot's not alone out there. Elon Musk has a project he calls Optimus.[6] It's a humanoid-looking robot with two arms and two legs. He believes, and I think he's right, that it could transform manufacturing as we know it. These robots will be used to put cars together before long, and what they'll be good at initially are dirty, repetitive, dangerous jobs that human beings don't want to do.

Even without investing in a robot, we have amazing capabilities to improve safety right in our pocket. With wireless technology and devices equipped with sensors, the old canary in the coal mine has been spared. We can now program digital sensors to measure temperature, oxygen content, humidity, or the presence of a bad combination of gases. We can then send the results with a Bluetooth signal to people waiting at a distance and check the data sent to their handheld device to determine if entering a space is safe.

THE BATHTUB CURVE

Predicting asset reliability can be somewhat challenging since it's an abstract concept. We're forced to put together statistics and performance data such that it will determine the likelihood of failure in the future. Once we're able to identify the presumed failure point, we can stay ahead of the curve by performing maintenance or procuring a replacement. Enterprise asset management (EAM) systems provide a number of predetermined key performance indicators (KPIs), while also allowing for custom KPIs. With a rich history of data in a system, we'll be able to identify asset performance and compare it to its life-cycle trend, which gives us the ability to manage utilization across our asset portfolio.

The Bathtub Curve

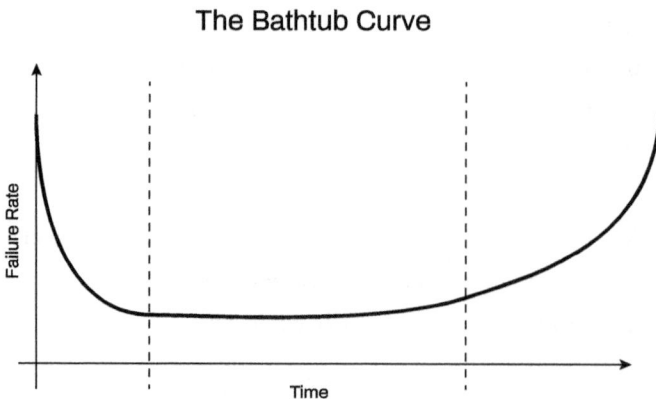

The maintenance industry has identified a trend called a "bathtub curve." A bathtub curve is the observed failure rate of any given piece of equipment, which combines three distinctly different trends in failure rate over time:

- Early failure

- Constant failure, or any set of random failures

- End-of-life failure

The combined, or observed, failure rate resembles the cross section of a bathtub. Essentially, the bathtub curve maps out the fact that early failure in equipment decreases as defective units and parts are replaced or weeded out. The useful life of the equipment maintains a constant low rate of failure. The failure rate then quickly increases at the end of the equipment's useful life. While this isn't necessarily a perfect analysis for all instances of failure, it works generally, and it can help apply KPI data to pinpoint the effort and cost associated with each piece of equipment within its life span.

In fact, many times if a machine is operating properly, invasive maintenance should be avoided for as long as possible. Often, if you tear a piece of equipment apart and put it back together, it's never going to be as good as it was when it was assembled in a clean room or a precision assembly line. The failure rate of that device will actually go up because of the invasiveness of the maintenance. You can monitor vibration and do thermal imaging to see hotspots, and you can track this data in your system. By comparing the performance data to the bathtub curve, you can be sure not to introduce invasive maintenance more often than necessary. This will lead to an extended useful life for the equipment.

A lot of maintenance procedures historically were based on time—performing maintenance monthly, quarterly, or semiannually. Maintenance schedules based on calendars don't take utilization into consideration, and can unnecessarily increase invasive maintenance, shortening the useful life of the assets. Certain regulated products, such as pharmaceuticals, may have a mandated maintenance schedule, often related to the quantity of an item produced, such as cleaning a machine after every one hundred thousand capsules. Usually, those regulated maintenance schedules are based on data or past experience as to where and when the potential for failure is likely to occur.

For example, the airline industry knows after decades of collecting and analyzing data that a fuel pump has a life span. They know how many hours of total flying time the pump will last. The FAA has specifications that outline when the fuel pump has to be removed from the aircraft for maintenance—it may be a certain number of takeoffs and landings or total number of hours in the air, but whichever threshold is met first, the maintenance must be performed, or the airline will be fined. And because of that predictive maintenance schedule based on real-world data, aviation in the United States today is very safe.

In my opinion, unregulated industries should take the approach of doing maintenance when it's necessary. That comes from collecting the correct information. If a pump is running fine, leave it alone. If you run vibration analysis on your mechanical equipment and you see that your pump is starting to vibrate, you know it might have a bad bearing, or be out of balance, or the coupling could be going. Something is outside of the norm, and now you have a reason to do maintenance. And that reason is most often based on two factors: value and criticality.

If you have a maintenance management system, you can track actual utilization and set up maintenance workflows accordingly. By taking feedback from the equipment, you'll be able to get from your system a predictive maintenance program.

Your system keeps you informed and up-to-date on all aspects of your maintenance program. Systems use numerical values to indicate priority for work orders, assets, and locations, and KPIs can show you where you fall on the bathtub curve. This allows you to determine the optimum maintenance schedule and enables you to establish cost-effective workflows. Using KPIs, the system software algorithm prioritizes effort, which allows your enterprise to maximize reliability at the lowest cost possible.

PREDICTIVE TOOLS

Success is about having the right preventions. The calendar is not preventa-tive. It's what the conditions are. If there is a condition that gives you reason to think, *Preventively, we want to shut this thing down*, you've got to have data points to support the trigger to do the preventative action. You got to have something concrete to apply your ounce of prevention.

Thermography is another very helpful tool for mechanical systems. Similar to the way a home digital thermometer can read your body tem-perature just by pointing it at your forehead, you can walk the floor in a plant, point a thermography tool at equipment, electrical panels, and so on and see hotspots. Temperature kills everything; whether it's an elec-trical problem or a mechanical problem, if the temperature's up, there's reason to be concerned. Something is off, something people might not see, or smell, or even pick up with the touch of a hand. Of course, the operation of the equipment itself does generate a level of heat, but when you have heat above that expected level, it's breaking stuff down, and that could be a couple of metal parts rubbing together because they're not lubricated appropriately or aren't aligned correctly. Once the hotspots are identified, then you know that an inspection and possible invasive main-tenance is warranted.

If you're managing server farms, or even laptops or PCs in general, you can do a number of things that probably fall into the same category. Every six months you ought to look at the condition of your hard drive and deter-mine whether it needs to be defragged or not. A number of software-driven tasks and/or processes leave behind digital footprints, and basically these are the equivalent of electronic dirt and dust. After a while, there's too much of it, and it needs to be cleaned out so your computer can operate more effectively and efficiently. This will prevent a machine from locking up or a software product from blue screening because we haven't cleaned the cache or defragged the hard drive.

Invest in predictive processes. Temperature is certainly a big one, but vibration sometimes will give you a lot of indication about what's going on.

And with drones equipped with cameras, you can visually inspect so much more than you could have before.

MORE USES FOR VISUAL TOOLS

The cost of electronic devices has come down over the years, but the cost of storage also has dropped precipitously. That gives you a cheap space that you can do something other than store the written word. I'm a big fan of photography. Everybody's got a phone; everybody's got a camera on their phone. When you can take a picture of something, whether you describe it correctly verbally or not, passing along that image in some shape or form is almost invaluable, and a lot of people haven't taken advantage of that yet.

The term *work order* is common in asset management. You know you have a job or a task. Maybe there are multiple tasks on a work order. But anytime you have documented what needs to be done, there are three or four things that are going to be there: a date, the name of the person who did the work, the asset involved, and, more often than not, a location. Databases are very dynamic. If you attach a picture to a work order, you can find it in several ways: who took the picture, when or where they were taken, or what asset the image captured, for example.

Even getting to the information you need to document is easier with a camera-enabled device. Just snap a picture of a hard-to-see nameplate on an asset, and the photo provides the information you need with good quality.

TIME TO PIVOT

Cameras are now part of car technology as well, as companies develop automobiles that will drive themselves. Tesla first tried using LIDAR radar to help the car "see" through fog and smoke. They were trying to use methods of detecting road hazards and objects in the environment in ways that fell outside of the human senses of sight, sound, and smell. The problem they ran up against was that they were trying to feed this information into artificial intelligence. They wanted the artificial intelligence to think like a human being, but they were providing it with something that wasn't human.

So they pivoted to using cameras in Teslas for most of these exterior detection needs. They then spent their time and energy on teaching the vehicle to recognize what things are—to look at a Dalmatian and understand that it's a Dalmatian, or to look at a trash can and realize that it's a trash can. Instead of wasting energy on peripheral things that didn't matter, they instead are giving the cars superhuman eyesight combined with the ability to recognize what they are seeing and make split-second decisions.

Sooner rather than later, we're going to be safer with cars driving themselves than with humans driving cars because the car is not going to have the distractions that we have, and it's going to see better and react faster. It's just mathematics.

INFORMED RUN TO FAIL

The business model of run to fail makes reliability folks cringe, but the really bright guys on Wall Street will tell you that they can make money in that model. They'll tell you that they don't need a maintenance group because they're going to run that machine until it dies, and when it does, they'll just put a new machine on that pad, and run that one until it drops, too. They expect to make more money doing that than they can make by hiring three technicians to manage and maintain the equipment.

Commodity businesses such as concrete or rock and aggregate mining use huge expensive pieces of equipment, and they're paid by the ton. A lot of the time, the mentality is "run to fail" and then install a new one. If they turn it off for an hour to grease or repair it or manage or maintain it, that's eighteen tons of loss production, and that's not applicable, so they instead run it until it drops. They have spares lying around in the yard, and when something breaks, they install a new one. Rather than turn that equipment off and interrupt the transportation of their commodity, they can show numbers that say it's better just to run it until it drops—assuming they're smart enough to have the spare. As long as they have the backup.

I would argue that the way they're going to make the most money is by buying the most reliable equipment to put on the pad in the first place. How do you know which is the best one? Well, a good system software tool will tell you. If you're pumping liquids in a food processing plant, and those pumps have a ten-thousand-hour life in Wichita, Oklahoma City, and Denver but only last one thousand hours in Oxnard, California, why is that? It turns out to be the salt in the air from the ocean. The pump has a varnish on the windings of the motors. The caustic salt air ventilates the system, and the acid is bad for the varnish. The same motor, same pad, same process, built exactly the same way, lasts only a tenth of the time on the coast as it will inland. The run-to-fail model in Oxnard would not have figured that out unless they had data from Wichita with which to compare. You might think you're on top of the world in Oxnard, but without reliability data, you wouldn't know that the pump you're using is failing at a higher rate than alternative pumps. So, believe it or not, maintenance and reliability intelligence will even support the run-to-fail model.

Key Takeaways

- When designing, avoid paralysis by analysis. Keep the design team small and focused, and don't get lost in the details.

- Design teams need executive support, a dedicated note taker, access to people with experience, and concrete targets.

- Prioritize and focus on the assets that are truly critical.

- Failure is a learning opportunity, especially with regards to criticality.

- Use the bathtub curve and predictive tools to determine timing of preventive maintenance.

- Technology's advanced sensing capabilities are better failure detectors and predictive tools than human senses.

- Let data tell you when "run to fail" makes business sense.

CHAPTER 3

IT'S ALL
ABOUT PROCESS

*"Never make excuses. Your friends don't need
them and your foes won't believe them."*

—John Wooden

IS PROCESS CRITICAL? THE GOOD,
THE BAD, AND THE UGLY

A large organization needs processes for how to do things, how to fix things, and how to respond in different situations. A written process that is based on best practice backed up by data and that everyone understands and follows is critical. But the process has to stand up to the test of those three elements, or the organization's throughput and productivity will likely suffer, and so will their ability to collect and analyze data.

It's worth testing if people really do know the process and use it. If you take ten different people from a group of one hundred and ask, "How are calls recorded?" and they don't give you the same answer, you know you have a problem. If you don't have that, then you've got to build it, and then you've got to make it a religion. Many companies get this when it comes to issues like safety and security. If they ask an employee, "Whose job is security?," the answer will likely be "Everyone's job." This is because they've sat in so many meetings and that was the first question in every meeting. It's become a mantra that security is everyone's job.

In my organization, I take the same approach with reliability, and I encourage our clients to do the same. Whose job is reliability? It's everybody's job. The machine operator should know when the machine is not operating correctly. He should make the call, and he should know how that call is handled, dispatched, reacted to, and prioritized. Not only so the day-to-day operations run smoothly but also so that everyone can provide helpful input when it's time to improve. If something happens outside of the norm, after one of those unique events, you bring everybody together and say, "Okay, what went wrong? What went right? If this were to happen again, what would be a better way of handling this? What held up your crew? What would you have needed to get your job done better?" And you add those lessons learned back into the process. It's a constantly evolving, living process that gets better with time as you find the exceptions to it.

> **Whose job is reliability? It's everybody's job.**

GOOD PROCESSES MAKE GOOD DATA

I like to say that integration is really the automation of a business process across multiple systems. Duplicate data entry is inefficient. You're trying to save your people time and get them to focus on their work. Current business process documentation is important to achieve this. Well-documented business processes that the entire enterprise agrees upon make for efficient, cost-effective software integration projects. When companies want to share data between systems, typically they're trying to eliminate duplicate data entry or duplicate data.

Entering transactional data into one system, then handing off the data in one direction to another system is not unusual (unidirectional integration). Conversely, entering transactional data in both systems so data moves in two directions (bidirectional integration) isn't uncommon, either. Mismatched data can be challenging; the invoice that doesn't match the purchase order needs to be reconciled. What if the system says the invoice is fixed and the financial system doesn't agree? When the amounts differ, which system wins needs to be decided. There are dozens of things that have to be flushed out in order for a bidirectional, fully functional integration to take place. The issue boils down to identifying which information is of value, and which system trumps the other in the event of a discrepancy.

If you have a solid, well-documented business workflow that everyone understands, and it works consistently, it can be automated relatively easily. Without consensus on the process workflow, integration is nearly impossible. It doesn't have anything to do with bits and bytes. Integrating software applications is doable, provided you begin with a well-documented business workflow that everyone agrees upon. If your business workflow doesn't work well the way it is, you'll end up spending a lot of money just to speed up how poorly it works.

If you've got bad processes, I would say you've got bad information. If you take those processes and automate them, you're just going to get bad information faster. So, it's about the right processes done consistently, and then keeping an eye on those things that show themselves.

WHEN PROCESSES BACKFIRE

As important as processes are, it's important to know when they aren't working.

I worked with a large consumer goods company that chose to outsource procurement to one big, multinational company that sells everything from rags to 100 hp DC motors—anything and everything. The intent was to get better pricing and control by being standardized on one vendor to provide them with all their needs. They thought there would be a data tracking benefit, too, as the vendor's catalog already provided unique part numbers for everything they needed to purchase.

Six months later, we interviewed people about the new procurement process, and we found that the company's employees were getting creative and finding a variety of ways to buy something without going through that one vendor. For example, they could go around the vendor if they had an emergency need for a specific supply, so suddenly all sorts of things were labeled an "emergency." Others would create artificially short timelines for when they needed a supply in order to have a reason to not use the vendor. The amount of stockpiling that occurred was huge. If the vendor stocked one brand, but the employee preferred another, the employee would create an "emergency" situation in order to purchase the brand they wanted and would buy literally years' worth of that favorite brand while they could.

The employees' reasons for going around the procurement policy were varied—using an external sourcing group meant lost jobs in the company's procurement department, and some people resented the external vendor that cost their friend a job. Others just didn't want to change the way they had always done things or try a substitute product.

The company hadn't expected everybody to seek ways around the policy as opposed to embracing the policy. They went back and rewrote the rules two or three times. They'd find out how people were gaming the system and then issue a memorandum that employees couldn't do this or that anymore. It took several years, at a cost of upward of a million dollars, before they finally gave up on the idea.

This company was constantly changing the process and trying to clamp down on people. And is that really what their goal was when they started? Their goal was to provide an efficient and effective way to procure materials so they could be more effective in their jobs. But instead, inefficiencies abounded as employees circumvented the process and the company spent a lot of time trying to clamp down on these work-arounds. It was a different way to waste time, which wastes money. And not only that, all these different ways of going around the system caused the company to lose something else precious: the opportunity to collect good data. What little information they did collect was incomplete and inaccurate, and therefore useless. Sometimes, dictating the way things should be done brings unintended consequences. If you're always trying to get people to do something and they're not doing it, maybe you need to rethink your goal.

Similar problems with sticking too long with a noncritical process can play out on a much bigger scale, such as at the level of a company's philosophy. Take Tesla when it was struggling with the mass production of the Model 3, making only two thousand cars a week instead of the promised five thousand. Elon Musk's vision from the beginning was that there wouldn't be anybody in the factory—everything was going to be robots; everything was going to be automated. What he had to come to grips with was that there were some things that humans just did better. Artificial intelligence can be impressive, but as of now, people are still better than machines at quickly adapting to changes in their surroundings.[1] He had to go back and revisit his approach, keeping automation where it made sense and inserting the human element where needed.

KEEP THE ONLY PROCESSES YOU NEED— OUTSOURCE THE REST

I've seen a lot of companies spending a ton of time trying to figure out what to do with manuals. You buy equipment, and it comes with a thick book filled with wiring diagrams, instructions, troubleshooting, and so on. Some companies spend gazillions of dollars on scanning and coding and storing. It's all an enormous waste of time. Just get rid of it and shred it. It's not worth managing and maintaining. Today if I need to know something, I google it. I was trying to adjust the door height on my Tesla the other day, and there's a 38,000-page owner's manual on the car's main screen. Instead of bothering with that, I googled it and had my answer in forty seconds.

I did see an interesting system that worked for a facility. They had a large campus, with twenty buildings built over a dozen years. They had a room of drawings and old-fashioned blueprints. They couldn't get funding to digitize it all, so what they did was hire a co-op every quarter from the local university and had him sit outside the door of the blueprint room. Somebody came in and got a blueprint. When they brought it back, they handed it to this young person, who then scanned it and filed it. They only spent their time digitizing what was actually used. They were never going to need 80 percent of the blueprints. But it's probably a good idea to catalog the 20 percent that comes and goes.

We have to get over any discomfort with pulling how-to information from the internet. Reframing how we look at the internet can help. Of course, there's content that's fluff or unreliable, but when it comes to basic how-to information, at the end of the day Google and YouTube and TikTok are examples of the larger collective mind of millions of people working in the same space. Instead of discounting or fearing these sources of information, teach your people good internet protocol so they know how to recognize when they have quality information. Sharing knowledge is incredibly valuable.

I think the collective whole becomes much more valuable than anyone's individual library. In 2020, we launched MORE (Maximo Online Resources & Education), an online community of Maximo users and experts from all over the world.[2] Users have access to discussion groups to help them get ideas and answers from experts and their peers plus an electronic resource library filled with best practices. People can search by a software function, and they can also see groups based on their vertical markets, giving them the widest access to ideas that match their needs. For example, in the manufacturing human consumables market, someone who makes crackers may learn a better process from someone who makes cheese.

If we're not careful, we can even lose value by not sharing, or by overprotecting ideas.

Many people today think our way of protecting intellectual property is upside down. Patenting unique ideas served a purpose once upon a time, but it may no longer be practical or desirable moving forward. Elon Musk has made available all his battery technology, all his technology around how to charge cars, his charging systems, how they're built, how they're designed, how they're engineered, all his patents.[3] He shared all of this with every automobile competitor on the planet. Tesla exists to promote sustainable transportation for the world, and just having his own set of patents and holding on to them himself doesn't support that philosophy of changing the world to a more sustainable transportation mode. For Tesla, not only is it the altruistic, better good of "let's move the world along to electric cars," but Elon Musk probably also sees that Tesla is bringing a certain value and a certain edge that doesn't have to be tied to how they're doing things in one moment of time or the patents they hold. There's something else that's always going to keep them ahead, and that's what they invest in, and by keeping their processes open, they can always keep moving and keep changing.

When you have a great idea, it's worth thinking about whether it's better to share it than to keep it to yourself. If the idea is for the better good, whether that's reducing impact on the environment or increasing safety in manufacturing, then sharing information can make sense. The internet is the new medium, and sharing is embedded in how the internet works. We're all sharing things voluntarily or involuntarily on the internet, so it's worth rethinking whether the information you want to lock down is truly what differentiates your company. If you focus too much on safeguarding intellectual property rather than realizing the real value you bring to the table, you may not be growing and changing with technology as fast as you can.

For many software developers, sharing has always been part of the culture.[4] Linux, for the most part, is still open-source. The concept of the Linux operating system is that it would be open-source in order to be shared and built upon. Some say, "Well, if it's open-source, you can't trust it, because it hasn't been tested." My response is that if you've crowdsourced the development, then crowdsource the testing.

There's a latent benefit to that sharing. You don't even know what it might lead to, but if you don't share it, you're never going to find out. There are definitely risks to not sharing. We run into this problem when helping companies that try to collect data on their assets with several distinct automated systems, each running on a different system that is proprietary to the original equipment manufacturer (OEM). In one factory, there may be three or four different machine communication systems, and they're all locked down and can't talk to one another, keeping us from bringing information all into one place.

By being too proprietary with their systems, companies can frustrate customers to the point of reputational or even legal complications. Over the years, people have lost the ability to repair their equipment because the only way to troubleshoot the system's software is with a diagnostic tool only the OEM has access to, and on top of that, the OEM may void your warranty if you attempt any repairs yourself. John Deere is now in the spotlight for just such a situation.[5] Imagine if you were a farmer in rural Oklahoma and your several-hundred-thousand-dollar tractor breaks down while you're in the middle of trying to plow a field, the only person who can fix it is 1,600 miles down the road, it's going to cost $35,000 to ship it there, and you are days away from losing a year's crop. Does this situation make sense? That's a bad place for a closed system. Companies need to think carefully about where to draw the line between protecting intellectual property and customer satisfaction.

Key Takeaways

- Design processes that work with how people work and test your processes. Good processes make good data.
- Keep only the processes you need.
- Share information, and you'll reap benefits.

CHAPTER 4

CONSISTENCY IS KEY

*"Be more concerned with your character
than your reputation, because your character is
what you really are, while your reputation
is merely what others think you are."*

—John Wooden

COMPANIES WANT 100 percent reliability, all the time. They want their computer to tell them what's going to break next, but they can't get that answer if they don't feed the good data into the system. And often the culprit behind unsatisfactory data is inconsistency. You can give people all kinds of great tools, but if you don't teach them how to use them correctly, they can be looking at things differently. Any kind of recording of information, any consistency that can be brought to a system, is hugely important.

ELECTRONIC DATA COLLECTION FOR CONSISTENT INPUTS

Collection is better handled with an electronic device than it is by paper, and with a set of predetermined selections rather than write-in fields.

Whether on paper or on a device, anything input in a discretionary way has to be transcribed at some point, and there's always the potential for the meaning to get lost in translation.

Think about communication in general. How many different languages are there in the world? The experts guess around seven thousand, but even professional linguists can't agree, because there is so much variability in language.[1] Even when you look at one language, different countries and regions can have different words for the same thing, or different spellings for the same word, and those differences cause problems when collecting and analyzing data.

I was involved in an awkward Federal Aviation Administration (FAA) audit once. We went into the audit thinking our system was ready to help answer the questions we'd be asked. One safety issue for all airlines is bird strikes—you'd be amazed how many times a bird collides with a plane in a given week. During the audit, the FAA asked how many bird strikes we'd had during the last reporting cycle. We looked at each other and thought, *No problem! That's such a softball!* But when we ran the query, we found ourselves with this challenge: Is *bird strike* one word, or two? A lot of people from New York will spell *bird* B-Y-R-D—how many different spellings could be in the system? And what if there was simply a typo? On top of that, we found that mechanics had many ways to describe how a bird might impact a plane—bird-incursion, hit-by-bird, plane-struck-bird—and typing in *bird strike* wouldn't catch those entries when you queried the system. The question ended up being a curveball, and the FAA knew it.

The solution is to eliminate free-form text fields and replace them with a selection field offering a limited set of descriptions. It's worth thinking through all of the areas for variability when setting up a system and trying to systematize the inputs whenever possible. That way, you're most likely to get out of your system what you put into it.

DEFINITIONS SUPPORT CONSISTENCY

There are many variables companies may want to track that at first seem hard to quantify. Sometimes the best approach is to simplify all the possibilities down to the most important question.

> **Sometimes the best approach is to simplify all the possibilities down to the most important question.**

Take planned versus reactive work, for example. Many companies have a goal to improve efficiency by making as much of their maintenance work planned work as they can. Let's say a boiler needs maintenance. The company knows the work involves removing the head of the boiler, getting a tubing machine in there, cleaning the tubes, replacing two or three of them, putting it all back together, installing new gaskets on it, putting the door back on, pressure testing it, and turning it on. All that takes two people about a day and a half. But you have to plan. You have to have the manpower, parts, and equipment available. If, on the other hand, the boiler springs a leak and needs immediate repair, it becomes an emergency situation. The same work has to be done, but because it wasn't planned for, the availability of manpower, the availability of parts, and the necessary equipment are all in question, and the amount of time, and likely money, it takes to perform the same task grows.

More time and energy are spent doing reactive work than planned work. Most people understand that. But defining planned versus reactive work is often up for interpretation. Knowing that planned work is preferred, people start playing semantics and say things like "Well, we were planning to do it. It happened a little sooner than we wanted it to, but since it was on our list to do eventually, we could still call it planned work." That makes for muddy datasets, in turn making it difficult to track the true efficiencies gained around planned maintenance.

When working with Cargill, I found it intriguing that they identified a simple way to cut through the semantics and give a definition to planned versus reactive work. They stated that for work to be considered planned, the team had to have at least a specific number of workdays' advance notice to perform that work. That gave them clean data. The number of days was defined by the team, and everyone was aware of it. Therefore, they knew what type of work was in the "planned work" category, and everything else was labeled reactive work. That made their workforce utilization comparison numbers trustworthy. Also, with a clear definition, employees began to think ahead—knowing that planned work was preferred and that seven days was the cutoff, the planning actually started happening earlier.

If you have something you want to track that seems difficult to quantify or suffers from murky datasets, create a simple definition.

MACHINE COLLECTION CAN REINFORCE PROCESS

In addition to making it easier to know that all of the data you are collecting will be consistently reported, automating data collection can help you see whether processes are being followed. Let's return to our HVAC company owner Ainsworth and see how dragging his feet on automatic data collection allowed a temperamental employee, Dale, to take a few costly liberties.

Ainsworth has a contract with a large medical research facility, and he's assigned Dale to collect data on a regular basis regarding the performance of the facility's chillers. Dale goes out to the site with clipboard and pencil in hand to note the temperature and pressure readings, plus document about fifteen more pieces of information, on about a dozen units. All in all, it takes him about two days to gather all the information from every unit.

Ainsworth felt that Dale's paperwork was a little sloppy. He decided to upgrade and bought digital thermometers for his team to use, hoping that would make it easier for Dale and his peers to be more precise.

Everyone's paperwork did improve with more precise temperature readings. With a digital win under his belt, Ainsworth decided to embrace a bit more technology and put tracking devices on his fleet of trucks, an upgrade his dispatcher had been asking for. Now, when a call for emergency work came in, Ainsworth's dispatcher could quickly find out which mechanic was closest and get someone there quickly.

One day, an emergency call comes in from a client just a mile away from the medical research facility where Dale is supposed to be working. Ainsworth tells the dispatcher to send Dale but is surprised to find out that the tracking signal from Dale's truck shows him to be across town. They dispatch someone else, and Ainsworth thinks nothing more about it until he reviews all of his mechanics' paperwork at the end of the week. Dale turned in a stack of forms with temperature readings from the chillers at the medical research center, including on the day they know his truck was somewhere else. Ainsworth decides to investigate.

He pulls Dale's paperwork from the medical research facility for the last several months. One easy measurement Dale is supposed to record is the ambient temperature. Ainsworth goes on the internet, checks the weather records, and sees that what Dale noted doesn't match the actual temperature for that day. Ainsworth starts checking more. He spreads out several years' worth of readings Dale has taken from the chillers at the medical research facility. Too many of the numbers for the different measurements Dale is supposed to be taking look identical from one year to the next. Ainsworth is pretty sure he knows why Dale's truck wasn't at the medical research facility the other day. He thinks Dale has simply been copying data from year to year, shortchanging his work, maybe even cutting out early. He doesn't know, but he's lost confidence in Dale's information.

He could fire Dale, but he's one of his most experienced mechanics. There are labor shortages, and the demand for Ainsworth's HVAC services are high. He thinks there might be a better way to get good data and put Dale on the type of service calls he excels at.

Ainsworth has been weighing whether or not to invest in installing thermistors—digital temperature sensors—on the chillers at the medical research facility. He decides it is time. With the thermistors in place, Ainsworth knows he's getting good data, and since the devices are enabled for Wi-Fi, Ainsworth's office staff can pull up the medical research facility readings remotely, and Dale can focus on actual repair work, only going out to the facility when something needs to be fixed.

Ainsworth's so pleased with what he's gained from these technological advancements that he decides to really dig into the capabilities of the software program that he installed when he put in the thermistors. He learns that he can set acceptable temperature ranges for the chillers at the medical research facility and the software will trigger an alert if the temperature rises above or falls below that range. He can then immediately send out a mechanic to see what may be causing the temperature anomaly. The software also allows Ainsworth to centralize data on his vehicles and his clients' HVAC systems into a network operations center. Now he's positioned for growth. He can definitely add a few more mechanics and trucks, but he's also heard that his long-time competitor, Jerry, is looking to retire. Ainsworth is ready to talk to Jerry about acquiring his company, doubling Ainsworth's business.

I've shown a compressed timeline for someone like Ainsworth realizing the value of progressively upgrading technology in a small business. But I believe Ainsworth's story is representative of the trajectory I've seen many companies take.

BE READY FOR THE LATEST TECHNOLOGY WITH GOOD DATA

Software is advancing at a very rapid rate with incredible capabilities, including some very futuristic abilities to predict things. It's like the commercial where the elevator technician shows up in a lobby of a high-rise building and says, "I'm here to fix the elevator." The gentleman at the building says, "There's nothing wrong with the elevator." The elevator technician says, "Well, there's going to be in two or three hours."[2] That's the dream for reliability professionals—to predict a problem and proactively fix it—and many see artificial intelligence and other advancements as the way to deliver that dream.

At Projetech, we have customers who watch similar commercials and then come to us asking for that same capability. And who can blame them? Imagine the cost savings if maintenance was always preventive and could be scheduled at the optimal time. The problem is, those same customers often don't have the information to support that new device or software's capabilities. If the data is fraught with error, you're not ready. You've got to get your processes squared away so that things are being done consistently, time and time again. Once you have consistently accurate data, then tools like machine learning and artificial intelligence are achievable.

I believe that this technology fundamentally flips our perspective on its head. The right people with the proper tools should respond to the assets that tell them exactly what needs to be done and when to do it. It's a much more intelligent approach to maintenance, making our traditional way of managing assets appear backward.

The theory is that if we just left the intelligent assets to manage their own needs, then they could be more reliable, and we wouldn't go ahead with unnecessary invasive maintenance. Quality machines integrated with a system will tell you not only what to do and when to do it but also every-thing you need to know about them: wire diagrams, parts lists, procedures, and the history of who has worked on it. Imagine the day that you can walk up to a machine, and it greets you by saying, "Hi, how are you doing? I'm a three-quarter horsepower pump. If you click here, I'll tell you the name of every mechanic who ever touched me. If you click over here, I'll tell you any temperature I've run at over the last five years within a tenth of a degree. If you click here, I'll give you an exploded view schematic so you know how to tear me down. Here's my spare parts list." It's quite the epiphany to appreciate just how much opportunity our current technolog-ical capability offers. Connected assets will soon be in the driver's seat for maintenance and reliability.

Key Takeaways

- Electronic data collection aids consistency.

- Defining terms makes it easier to collect consistent data.

- Digital data systems can show you whether processes are being followed.

- Artificial intelligence and other advanced technology require good data to work.

CHAPTER 5

REACTIONS TO CHANGE

"Failure is not fatal, but failure to change might be."

—John Wooden

LEADERS IN ANY company know that change is a part of business. That's nothing new. But what feels different today is how fast change is coming at us. Regardless of whether you manage people or processes, or whether your company makes widgets or serves up experiences for customers, the pace of change in our world has accelerated. Many businesses that once could operate for decades doing things the same way now find themselves pivoting every year as they respond to changes in their midst, changes that are often spurred by constantly evolving technology.

I always refer to people, processes, and technologies as the three-legged stool of the maintenance and reliability industry. And when it comes to technological change, people are as integral a part of it as the process. Technology is driving the speed of change, and when people don't have the skills to keep up or when they are averse to change, it causes some challenges.

In our business of helping people better manage their assets through technology, we're right there in the room when companies are grappling with change. However, rarely do they walk in the door saying, "I want change."

When they come to us, what's on their mind is improvement. They want something to affect their business positively, and whether that's decreasing downtime, reducing waste, boosting production numbers, or increasing quality, that something usually boils down to improving reliability. To become more reliable, you need information. That information must be collected in some fashion, and that usually involves some sort of process. And that process is going to involve change. Inevitably, change has to be part of getting better.

Improvement isn't a one-shot deal. Companies will always need to evaluate how they are doing, and they'll always find there is room to improve, which means that change will always be a part of their business. This is a journey, not a destination. It's a marathon, not a sprint. It's something you impart to a company. Constant improvement. Constant re-evaluation. Constant change. Learn, change to improve, repeat. That's business today.

> **Learn, change to improve, repeat.**
> **That's business today.**

Over the years, I've had a front-row seat to the work of over a thousand companies across a wide range of industries trying to change for the better. And I can distill all the leaders' reactions I've seen into a couple of broad categories. There are the leaders who are naturally averse to change and who'll go to the ends of the earth to avoid it. Then there are those who thrive on change. I'll admit, that's me. I don't mind a little chaos, as long as we're channeling it toward improvement. And I've seen leaders who fall somewhere in the middle of that spectrum of hating or loving change.

WHO OWNS THE IDEA?

In addition to their personal tendencies, how a leader reacts to change often relates to whether change was that leader's idea. If they're the instigator, their opinion of change is going to be better than if it's forced on them. But regardless, the company leaders have to show they are committed to the change at hand. It can't be lip service. You've got to have buy-in and visible participation from the top down.

Since change is an essential part of business today, it's worth it for leaders to take a look in the mirror and see how they react to change in general or how they feel about the change they're grappling with at the moment. How the leader approaches change has a lot to do with whether the company will see improvement or get bogged down in a bit of a mess. From what I've seen, the personal feelings leaders have about change manifest into one of three reactions: fear of change, chasing the latest and greatest, or a measured and thoughtful approach. Let's take a look at each.

FEAR OF CHANGE

Believe it or not, there are still a lot of companies out there that rely on paper and writing things down by hand for most of their reliability systems. I grew up in the contracting business, what many refer to as the typical trades companies. And in those industries, particularly in small- and medium-sized companies, reliability systems are often undermanaged, looking only at people's mistakes with processes that lack technology.

We're often brought in to help organizations at all different levels—it could be the business unit manager, or manager of the maintenance department, or even a plant manager who saw they could do something better and wanted help, but seldom would the call come from the top. And so, using technology to get better reliability would need to be sold up. If there was a fear of change, we'd run into resistance.

Oftentimes, we found leaders somewhat stuck in an antiautomation attitude. Over the years, I've heard many a person say to me, "I don't want my maintenance men sitting in front of a computer. I want them turning wrenches and doing what I hired them to do." Other times, we found organizations that, being unfamiliar with what technology could do for them, hadn't budgeted for the change their lower-level managers wanted to make.

To cut through the resistance, I'd ask the manager who wanted the change, "What is it that your leaders above you regularly ask for as part of your day-to-day business that you can't provide?" Often, that answer would be information. They want to know where they're spending their money—why it cost so much to fix something or why the manager wants to put another body on a shift. And we'd show how data collected by technology not only answers those questions but also gives them information about questions they hadn't even known they needed to ask.

Remember our friend Ainsworth with the HVAC company? We all know that cash flow is vital to a small- to medium-sized business. Ainsworth's not a big fan of technology, but he's got to get those invoices out the door quickly to get paid in time to take care of his bills. But Ainsworth's got a problem, and his name—you guessed it from what you've heard before—is Dale.

Now, Dale's been with the company for years. He knows his stuff, and his work is fantastic. But once he leaves the job site, the problems start. Dale's not consistent about completing his paperwork at the site before he leaves. Ainsworth is dependent on that paper to send out an invoice. How that paper gets back to the office is one challenge. How to ensure that it's done in a timely fashion? How do we know that the paperwork that has been received is accurate? If Dale procrastinates and does all his paperwork at the end of the week because he has to turn it in on Friday, he's doing things from memory, it's sloppy, and things get forgotten.

This is more than an inconvenience. Ainsworth's HVAC service business is essentially selling hours of the mechanics' time. But there are only so many hours to sell. There is a limit to how many hours a day Ainsworth's employees can work. So, Ainsworth's type of business lives and dies with material mark-ups. Now, let's see how that plays out as we follow Dale on a typical week.

Dale went out on Monday to a huge research facility for the week, working on various components of their HVAC system. Now it's Friday, and he's had several different jobs since then. He's trying to fill out his paperwork for the week, and he's remembering most of his work, but he's trying to think back to that research facility he did on Monday. He's foggy about how many hours he was there, but the more important thing is that he had to replace a large motor on an induction fan. He had miscellaneous materials and had to replace a defective switch, but the motor was under warranty, so there was no charge to the customer for that part.

Dale turns the paperwork in, and the office staff sees that there's no charge for the motor, but there's no way of tracking where the defective motor is or what happened to it. If it was a warranty motor, did it go back to the manufacturer for credit? Is it still sitting on the floor at the research center? That motor cost Ainsworth a thousand dollars, and if Ainsworth can't find it, he can't claim the warranty rebate from the manufacturer. Because there is no paper trail, Ainsworth has to go on the hunt to find that motor. He has to do it now, because the warranty is about to expire.

So, Ainsworth radios Dale, who is back out on a job, and he finds out that the motor is still rolling around in the back of Dale's truck because Dale didn't have the warranty claim form he needed. No one else can fill out the form because the knowledge of the motor and job are all in Dale's head. Ainsworth hates to do it, but he pulls Dale from the job and sends him back to the supply house to fill out the form, losing billable time for one of his best service employees. Dale bills at about one hundred dollars an hour, and it takes half a day for him to get back in, fill out the form, and then get to his next job. And until Dale gets there, the office personnel are paralyzed, not able to process the paperwork they need to. When you add up the cost of office personnel sitting idle and Dale's lost billing hours, that nearly eats up the one thousand dollars that Ainsworth will get back in the warranty claim from the motor manufacturer.

Added to that, typically Dale isn't just careless about one defective motor. Dale often grabs the wrong part because he doesn't check the paperwork closely enough. Or he has a stack of half-completed expired warranty claim forms stashed in the glove compartment of his truck that he's forgotten about. Or any number of mistakes that seem small to Dale but add up for Ainsworth. Dale becomes Ainsworth's biggest money-making and biggest money-losing employee, all at the same time.

Ainsworth realizes that about one in four of his service employees are like Dale. His back-office staff has grown because more people are needed to sift through the chaos created by a quarter of the service force not adhering to process and everyone is relying on human memory and spending time pushing paper. Once we lay out all of the expenses Ainsworth is racking up that can be reduced with an automated electronic system, even a technology-resistant leader like Ainsworth can see why change has to happen.

STREAMLINE YOUR SYSTEMS

Over time, we've seen more and more leaders like Ainsworth be willing to make a change and invest in digitizing their processes and asking good questions to learn what they can from the data they're collecting. They're now asking, "We have all of this technology; why can't I see better information? Where are my people? And exactly how much wrench time am I getting out of them?" Often those questions come up because there are too many systems, each tracking a separate thing—one for wrench time, one for travel, and so on. To get better data, the company needs to streamline and consolidate its systems. And what we find is that the resistance to change has moved down the line from the leader to the workforce. Whether it's a change from filling out a form on paper to doing it on a phone or tablet, or a change from logging their time in one system rather than another, it's hard for workers who have done things a certain way for most of their career to make a change.

I've always said that if you tie using the process to the employee's pay, you'll get better information. It'll be exactly right—you worked eight hours; you'll get eight hours of documentation. If you don't tie the work performed and the pay systems together, often you'll get eight hours logged on the time card but only six and one-half hours of work documented, and that leaves you with a discrepancy.

We have to understand where the employee is coming from. People don't like their paychecks being messed with. And there can be other factors. For example, for a unionized workforce, there are union rules and regulations around time recording that the union has negotiated trying to protect their members from being overworked. If you come in with some grandiose scheme to better handle information to better document what's being done, more often than not you're going to be in violation of some union rule. It's not as simple as making a change in a system or making a change to a process; you have to go all the way back to labor contracts and start there. Changing human behavior is difficult enough, but when you have work rules that conflict with that change, the difficulty is just multiplied.

MANAGING CONFLICT TO DRIVE CHANGE

These conflicts can come up in places other than pay. For example, there can be internal conflict between operations and maintenance. The maintenance people have been tasked to do something, to perform a repair or routine maintenance. But the department has an operational goal of making one thousand widgets today. In order for the maintenance man to do his job, you've got to turn off the line that produces those one thousand widgets. Those competing goals create friction.

Sometimes the resistance to change isn't related to an emotional reaction or the need to define priorities. Sometimes it's coming from the logical place of realizing that the cost of the change isn't worth the savings the new system will bring.

However, some of those same issues can be used as leverage points to drive change. Let's take the concern about paychecks as an example. Compensation is a great way to overcome resistance to change. I know a recycling company that was having a hard time getting its maintenance staff to switch to digital processes. So, they decided to implement the change in phases, starting with the least entrenched aspects of their workforce. They rolled out the new system first to contractors. Anybody who came on-site to do work for them was required to document their work the new way. At the same time, they made the new process a condition of employment. All the new people who came in through the door were taught the new system.

Then, for the older crew, the company recognized that the individual employee didn't receive any value for changing the system. They were focused on doing their jobs. They were getting paid by the hour to fix things, and that's what they did. They didn't see any need to document what they did. If something wasn't broken, they were doing their job. If it was broken, they had to go out and get it to work. But writing it all down and keeping track of it just didn't make any sense to them. They didn't think there was any money in that. So, the company gave an incentive to adopt the new system at annual review time. They'd say to an employee, "You're making twenty-eight dollars an hour. I'd really like to give you twenty-nine, but I can't do it until I can get you onto this new system."

For that company, it also helped when they could show how documenting work saved the company money. Picture this recycling company; it's like a big junkyard. Trucks are coming and going constantly, dumping loads of steel and copper. In the midst of all of that, contractors come in to fix cranes and backhoes or work on vehicles or air-conditioning, or whatever else needed to be done. But every truck must pass through the guard gate.

The company was convinced that they were being billed incorrectly by contractors. So, they changed their process and made contractors fill out a form at the guard gate when they checked into the site, and then complete the form at the gate as they left the site, noting the work performed and the time spent. Their contractor cost dropped dramatically in the first six months, even before the company had looked through the paperwork they'd been collecting. The fact that the contractors were filling out that paper made them think that somebody was looking at it immediately, and suddenly, the quality of the data went up.

CHASING THE LATEST AND GREATEST

Sometimes people jump into change too quickly. The software industry has pretty much programmed us to keep up with the Joneses. The next version of Microsoft or Maximo comes out, and because there are versions and because they're numbered, it's a status thing to have the most current one.

Ironically, in my opinion, a lot of what's in the newer products are simply fixes of deficiencies in the prior products, but there are typically some new functional things that are marketed heavily that make people want to jump in and be early adopters. Some of them are very successful with that, and others are simply bleeding-edge victims who move too fast and spend a lot of money unnecessarily.

When you are deciding whether or not you want to be an early adopter, think again about the "top three things" principle. What do you want to get out of it? What are the three value propositions that make this a good business decision? Then sit down and have a serious talk with yourself about whether you actually have the ability to leverage that value. For example, let's say you want to use artificial intelligence (AI). Well, you're going to need to have a lot of good data for AI to be helpful. So, do you truly have good data? Good enough to invest the money to apply AI to it?

The medical industry provides a good example.[1] Whenever a medical study is done, a lot of data is generated. AI has the potential to take that data and process it, with an accuracy in the mid-90 percentile range, interpreting that data to provide useful suggestions.[2]

However, the medical industry is currently having a difficult time leveraging AI because of the way medical workers currently write their research. For example, they conduct studies with a thousand people, and they use a placebo. Then human beings interpret that data, and more often than not, they share it using written words. The written form makes it very difficult to aggregate that information in an accurate way. Recently, IBM sold off their medical AI business, and in my opinion, it was for this very reason that the inability of a computer to interpret human language and understand *written* medical data made it practically impossible for them to achieve what they were trying to do.

The problem is that all the current medical data is in different formats, and massive amounts of it are in the written word as opposed to being digital. When you're trying to aggregate ten thousand cancer patient records, for example, language barriers, spelling errors, and other issues will preclude you from getting accurate information. Written words that have been scanned have an accuracy of only about 70 percent when processed, a loss of over 25 percent accuracy compared to analyzing data that was digitally collected.[3] If the health-care industry adopts digitization, we have an opportunity to advance treatments and the search for cures because more accurate data will be all in one place for the best use of the doctors in charge.

EARLY ADOPTERS

The people Malcolm Gladwell calls "early adopters" in his book *The Tipping Point* are important. They shake out a lot of issues that might not have been prevalent during development. But should you be one? I think that depends on whether you are genuinely interested in the technology. If you're ready to spend the seventy or eighty hours a week needed to understand it and make it work and tinker with it and really get into the underpinnings and understand why it's structured the way it is and why it does what it does, then you'll learn something valuable.

One of my favorite early adopters was the University of Dayton, located in Ohio just north of Cincinnati. In the 1990s, they decided to put PalmPilots in the hands of their mechanics. Today, people walk around with smartphones in their hands. But at the time, they were years ahead of people. They gathered data on the PalmPilots and then put the device in a charging dock at the end of their shift, where the content was also downloaded (this was before Wi-Fi). It really improved their data gathering and wrench time.

Now we carry around an amazing amount of computing capability every day in our pocket. Being able to have a device with you at all times that can take a photo has made a big difference in the reliability world. Once, when I was on an airplane, an inexperienced tug operator was operating the tug that pushes the plane into position. The tug operator somehow made the tug lurch forward and dented the nose of the plane.

Quality inspectors were staring at the nose of the plane. Taking off the nose is a big piece of work—the flight has to be canceled, and the plane goes back to the hangar. They call in the problem and say, "Well, we've got a bump in the dome. We want to know if we can fly the plane." A lot of time is wasted trying to measure the dent and relay information about the condition of the nose over the phone.

Finally, somebody decides to take a picture and send it to the decision maker on the other end of the line. Quickly, they decide the dent isn't too bad, and they can fly the plane. That would have been a great end to the story, except the same tug operator gets back in the tug and dents the nose of the plane again, only worse this time. After hours of making passengers wait, the flight is finally canceled. But, from the maintenance end, they figured out they could save time by using the phone in their pocket.

GOING DIGITAL ENHANCES ACCURACY

A company founded in the early 1970s and based in Newfoundland produces an impressive 130,000 barrels of oil per day. It also exports nearly 90 percent of its petroleum products to international markets mainly throughout Europe and the United States.

With 5,000 locations, tracking, maintaining, and documenting work is essential to the organization—but it was mainly only being done on paper. Needless to say, this increased the difficulty of organizing and retrieving stored records and data recording, and it resulted in missing data, as well as trouble managing assets.

By switching from a paper to a digital system, the company resolved the vast majority of these issues very quickly. Its operators now use tablets on their rounds to upload readings into the maintenance management system, enabling all operator rounds' tasks to be visible in the system.

The search functionality allows the company to easily search for historical data, track changes over time, and find anomalies before they even cause a problem. Another benefit is that, because the system

continued

can be synchronized offline, operators can work even when they are not connected to the internet. The enhanced accuracy provided by the digital system allowed the company to make more informed decisions regarding their assets and operate at a more efficient level.

DOING CHANGE THE RIGHT WAY

Creating change through technology works best with a measured approach with a group that knows what they want to get out of the work. That group needs to have all of the pieces in place: the right people, including a project manager with experience keeping a group on task; reasonable expectations; a budget; a timeline; and visible executive support. In addition to those must-haves, there are some approaches that will set the team up for success that relate to how the team approaches designing the system, how to make sure the system will deliver the information you've captured in a way that you can use it, and how to keep the system safe, secure, and ready for what may come in the future.

Key Takeaways

- People are an integral part of technological change.
- When people ask for change, what they usually want is improvement.
- Improvement is a journey, not a destination.
- Leaders set the tone for how change will be perceived in their organization.

- Learn what motivates people to overcome their fear of change.

- Know when it makes sense to be an early adopter—when you get value from the change and when you can leverage the change—and when it makes sense to wait.

- Do change the right way by having a clear idea of what you gain from the change and supporting the change team with a healthy budget, a timeline, and executive support.

CHAPTER 6

PREPARE FOR THE UNEXPECTED

*"If you're not making mistakes, then you're not doing anything.
I'm positive that a doer makes mistakes."*

—John Wooden

WHILE IT'S TRUE that you install a new and sophisticated software technology with the expectation that it will add great benefits to your company, there can also be unanticipated impacts resulting from that investment. No one can tell the future, so you can't possibly foresee all the angles when you introduce a complex system. When you implement this technology and take a hard look at your processes and your people, you'll likely uncover a few surprises.

For example, when you first include inventory in a system, you may realize that you have hundreds of thousands of dollars' worth of spare parts on the shelf, many of which have been there for years. Consider the fact that for a long time, you've paid taxes on this inventory that could be obsolete, and then there's the real estate the inventory is taking up in your storage area.[1] For some companies we've worked with, the carrying cost of obsolete inventory ran into the millions of dollars. Research shows that this is often the case in many companies.[2]

IMPROVING OPERATIONAL EFFICIENCIES THROUGH A UNIFIED SOLUTION FOR INVENTORY

One of the nation's largest personalized digital media networks for grocery, mass, and drug retailers with operations in the United States, Europe, and Japan was unable to get parts when and where they needed them. Consequently, they needed to find out where the failures were. The company needed a streamlined software solution to reconcile its four separate systems to identify the assets' location, whether it was online or offline. It has nearly four hundred thousand rotatable printer assets in its inventory and four systems to manage fixed assets, inventory, client locations, and data warehouse print logs. The organization was in desperate need for an innovative method to unify its many moving parts.

Projetech's cloud-based Maximo provided the industry leader with a unified solution to manage and locate all inventory parts at each of its vendors and track failures across the entire network. Having 24/7 access to a team of Maximo specialists, a client help desk, and MaaS's cloud-based model also eliminated the high cost required for servers or an on-site database administrator. MaaS streamlined their receiving process by scanning the asset's barcode, allowing the company to save on costs and free up resources by reducing the time required to receive and sort each new printer from approximately three minutes to thirty seconds.

Through Maximo, the organization was able to decipher which printers were defective—saving time, money, and manpower. It enabled them to calculate the impact of downtime and repair costs of these defects on their bottom line. The information provided by Maximo also helped hold printer manufacturers accountable for product failures and report accurate failure rates. In fact, they could quantify that the printers had a 50 percent annualized failure rate, and that was clearly unacceptable in any industry.

The data provided by Maximo was extremely valuable because it allowed them to negotiate better deals with printer manufacturers and focus on business continuity instead of system infrastructure and maintenance.

We've seen companies uncover a lot of interesting hidden inefficiencies, one of which can best be described by checking back in with our friend Ainsworth with the HVAC company. Ainsworth has already learned that tracking his fleet of trucks can verify whether his crew is where they are supposed to be. He decided to put his system to work and also track information that could tell him how his crew's driving habits were affecting the wear and tear on his fleet. Repair bills were up, and Ainsworth had to replace four trucks this year alone, costing him over $100,000. He hoped that with better data, he could home in on the employees who needed training on how to take better care of his trucks. While he was at it, Ainsworth decided to track gasoline use as well.

After a few weeks, Ainsworth had the data he needed and pulled a few mechanics in for reminders on how to properly care for the vehicles, some of whom he put on probation until their driving habits improved. But there was one set of numbers he thought must be wrong. Dale's truck was only getting three miles to the gallon. *Three*. Ainsworth thought it had to be a mistake, that someone must have put in a wrong number somewhere. He

watched the gasoline usage numbers for another week and couldn't deny that the pattern was there.

Ainsworth thought back to the time when the vehicle tracking system showed that Dale wasn't at the medical research facility when he was supposed to be. He pulled that record and looked at the address. On a hunch, he compared the address with the one in Dale's personnel file, and they matched. Dale had skipped work, that day at least, and gone home. Most of Ainsworth's mechanics did drive the company trucks home at night, but they weren't supposed to use them for personal reasons. Ainsworth wondered if Dale had figured some way to rig the mileage reported for the trucks to cover up the fact that he was driving company trucks on personal time. He decided to find out.

That evening, Ainsworth dropped by Dale's home not long after he should have arrived after the end of his day's work. As he pulled up, he saw that the company truck was parked in Dale's driveway like it should be, and Ainsworth wondered if he'd been wrong. But as he got closer, he saw the reason the gas mileage was so poor for that one truck. There was Dale, standing between the company truck and his personal car, holding a hose running between the two vehicles' gas tanks. Dale was siphoning gas out of the company truck to fill up the tank of his own car. It was the last straw. Ainsworth fired Dale.

Not all surprises come from exposing hidden costs or problems. For example, all sorts of service businesses have been finding they can reduce costs while providing customers with a premium level of service.[3] Think about the rental car companies that allow you to go right to a ready and waiting car. That cuts down on their personnel costs. Today, there are rental car companies that have taken the concept a step further. They just take a picture of your driver's license, completely eliminating human interaction in the rental of a vehicle.

Or take dry cleaning. It used to take several days for the dry cleaner to return your clothes until several companies started offering same-day or overnight service. By offering a quicker turnaround, they became more efficient. Their throughput went up, customer satisfaction went up, and the cost of goods sold went down.

TAKING IT TO THE NEXT LEVEL

Today, companies have taken that to the next level. I'll give you an example from the two places where I split my time: Florida and Ohio. In Florida, my dry cleaner was very conveniently located—right on the corner of my block—and was one of seven small retail storefronts this group owned. When the COVID-19 pandemic happened, neither I nor anyone else could go into the dry cleaner's store anymore, and I think they were in danger of going out of business. They started contacting people by either mail or phone, saying, "Hey, you can't come to our store anymore, but we're going to come pick up any laundry that you need to have dry-cleaned."

They started doing valet dry cleaning, and four months later they closed all their retail stores. Now they're completely virtual. They always had one cleaning operation for those seven storefronts, and they kept the cleaning operation, but now there's no human touch—I've not seen my dry-cleaning valet guy in years—and because of that, a big expense they had with rent and retail employees just went away. That change didn't just save the business—it also probably made it one of the more profitable businesses around.

In Ohio, when the COVID-19 pandemic happened, my favorite pizzeria, which is a part of a franchise, had to eliminate dining room service. So there were no more bussers, no waitresses who didn't show up for their shifts, none of the cleaning and the dishes and all that stuff; now all they were doing was shoving a pie out a window. Once people were allowed to dine out again, these pizza franchises begged their corporate office not to open up the dining rooms again, because they were saving so much money without them. There's a lot of money in a pizza pie. Especially if you can get somebody to pull up in a car and deliver it to them out a window and take a credit card, the margins are crazy good as opposed to having a dining room that requires cleaning, employees who don't show up, and customers who complain. If you can cut all of those costs and make a pie for three bucks and still charge twenty, that's a very lucrative business.

WHAT DRY CLEANING AND PIZZA CAN TEACH YOU

I think there are three lessons that any business can learn from my dry cleaner and pizzeria. The first lesson is that when you do have change forced upon you temporarily, don't just automatically revert to the old ways when the situation goes back to "normal." Think about whether this is a chance to improve your business model. The second lesson is that, as technology is increasing, don't wait for a catastrophic change to force you to be different. See if that technology does something for your business model, or you may be leaving a lot of money on the table. And the third lesson is that, as business models around you change, see if there is some longing customers have that you can help fill. In the case of my pizzeria, it's cheaper to not reopen the dining rooms, but at some point, people will want to get together and share meals again. That is something humans have always liked to do and probably always will. And so my pizzeria might invest in being the pizza place that has the best outdoor seating, such as an all-weather patio, in addition to a traditional dining room, curbside services, and delivery. As much as possible, all of those services can be virtualized. Customers walk up to the table and tap on a QR code, and the menu pops up on their phone. They order by tapping on their selections so no one has to wait on them. Somebody just facilitates the delivery of the food—or in some places, robotic waiters come rolling down the aisle with the meal, thus eliminating a lot of labor by reducing touch but still keeping the experience of dining out together that customers want.

> **Don't wait for a catastrophic change to force you to be different.**

There's an app for everything now, and there's a service for everything, too. In many ways, we've returned to a service world like we used to have when the milkman came to your house instead of you having to go out and buy milk at the grocery store, except now with greater speed and customization. Look at your business with a clean sheet of paper and say, "Okay, what if everything just happens on a phone?" Eliminating touch is a problem-solving opportunity, but if you forget completely the human touch side, somebody else is going to see that as a business opportunity and sweep in and take the lion's share of the customers. You've got to weigh it all and find a balance.

BE READY; BE PREPARED

For companies to respond to the demand for the next app-based service, they have to be ready with good, secure systems. After all, rental car companies can only remove the need for people to check that the person renting the car has a driver's license if they are confident that they have a secure way to view personal information.

I see logistics companies creating similar efficiencies when they eliminate warehousing at their distribution centers. They've updated their design so that a semi pulls into one end of the center and workers unload the goods directly onto a series of conveyors. Other workers sort the goods as they flow through the center, routing them to the right trucks waiting at the other end of the building to take the goods to the retail store.

Manufacturing has also seen changes. The just-in-time trend and the fact that manufacturers have become a lot more linear and integrated mean that the dependencies from one machine to another are greater today. That, combined with speed, has accelerated the criticality of key assets and being prepared for whatever could happen in production.

For example, back when a car manufacturer had a target of just a few hundred cars, they could afford to lose a particular pump for thirty or forty minutes before the entire assembly line came to a halt. The company would have spare pumps sitting right there with everything necessary to be able to replace it in less than thirty minutes, so there was no need to stop the line. Today that pump might be responsible for three concurrent lines running with a target of thousands of cars, and it can't go down for even ten minutes at a time because the speed of the system is that much faster. You have to look at the process itself. Car manufacturers probably should have more than one pump so that if pump A goes down, they can turn on pump B. It's just a different way of handling the problem.

I think flexibility is a factor, too. If you're making white cars and there's an order for red cars, you've got to change over from one to the other. How critical is it to do the paint booth maintenance tonight? If you need fifty red cars in the morning, can you make the red cars first and then the white? After all, what drives business is sales.

You don't want a fear of technology problems standing in your way. When you work with the internet, things happen. Let's go back to my dry cleaner in Florida for an example. The other day, the valet guy showed up and apologized for deliveries being screwed up because their internet was down the entire day before. The internet wouldn't have had this kind of impact on a dry cleaner even just two years ago. But I understood, because I didn't have internet service either during that time because the provider was out for the whole area.

Don't let the fear of those kinds of problems get in your way. Depending on what the issue is, your customers may go through the same experience or something similar enough that they know it's just part of how the world works right now. Essentially, your customers have the same technology you do. We all have Wi-Fi; we all have smartphones. We all know things happen. There's a little bit more wiggle room for mistakes with internet-based technology when customers experience the same problems and make a distinction between problems with the internet versus problems completely within a company's control. The internet is different than previous generations' technology, which everyday people didn't use themselves and couldn't replicate at home, such as when mainframes first came out.

BRIDGING THE GAP

Our personal use of technology and our commercial use of technology are closer together than they've been in the past. Consider video conferencing: We use it at work, and we use it at home to play online bridge with Grandma so that she has a connection with us. And if our internet goes out at home, we don't disappoint Grandma. We use a cell signal for our Zoom. If a storm or high demand brings the network to its knees, everybody just moves to some other way of connecting because they have options, and they know there are other ways to get online.

But in business, instead of preparing for an eventuality like internet disruption, we often fear it and let it keep us from trying new things. I've had customers over the years argue against cloud computing because they didn't believe that internet connectivity was reliable enough. One example of this is a city in the far northeast corner of Australia called Darwin. It's a small city and very remote. They needed a cloud solution for a very large management system; they were managing water for an area about the size of Texas. There weren't that many people, but it was a huge geographic area. They needed to move to the cloud—all of their system's data was housed in an old data center, and it was all trash—but they decided against it. Their argument for not moving to the cloud was that there was only one fiber connection between Darwin and the closest major city. They didn't want to move to using the cloud until they had more than one fiber feed—until they had backup redundancy. They said they didn't want to put all their eggs in one basket; they were afraid that if something were to happen, their entire maintenance management system would be down. But what they were ignoring is that if the fiber line went down, they would be out of the water delivery business completely. If they didn't have the internet, they weren't going to deliver water. If they didn't have internet, they weren't going to talk on the phone. If they didn't have internet, they weren't going to have electricity. Their maintenance management system being down would be the least of their problems.

INTEGRATION IS CRITICAL

So, whatever it is you're making, you're integrated now. Operations in the office building and the factory out in the field are usually very much closer together today. When visiting Toyota, I found it interesting that they put operations right in the middle of manufacturing. They share desks. The idea is that they could respond faster to needs or challenges. The engineering people, the manufacturing people, and the operations people are all sitting in the same room, and that interdependency with operations and engineering is critical.

Providers often automate processes to improve customer satisfaction or deliver their service at a higher price point. But if you have good data, you might find that you're saving money, too, by making your process more efficient. Be inquisitive and open-minded. Try to approach such unintended consequences with a curiosity mindset and see what opportunities arise.

As a service provider, I think the disruption that BYOD (bring your own device) creates lends an advantage to service providers. While many corporations are not prepared to deal with it, the cost of catching up is prohibitive. When mobile users can't connect with their company's resources by mobile, they feel an "app gap," as described in this 2013 study by Vanson Bourne:

> As organizations make plans to fill the app gap, they face some roadblocks. According to the research, perceived risks to implementing formal mobility strategies include security (54 percent), the additional investment required (48 percent) and the need for ongoing support (47 percent). In addition, more than half of companies (56 percent) are concerned that they lack the skills to develop an appropriate application and application interface across myriad mobile devices and platforms.[4]

With the evolution of technology, it's important to concentrate on what has not been done yet that has the potential to develop. It is also key to stay alert if there are business opportunities or changes coming in the future.

I don't think you're going to see this happen as a bow wave. Incrementally, you're going to start seeing small changes in the way things operate, little incremental improvements in how they get better. It will stair-step its way into manufacturing processes or transportation or anything else. The logistics people are really out in front on all this.

Look what Amazon has been able to do with next-day or same-day deliveries. And other companies were changing and using that same model. It really has to do with the connectivity of the transportation devices—the trucks, the trains, the airplanes—but also the ability to track the location of individual products. Most of us are kind of spoiled now; we order a Tommy Bahama shirt online, and tomorrow we can log on and track it. We know that it left Oxnard, California, at 11:00 p.m. last night, it's in Tennessee today, and it's supposed to be in Cincinnati tomorrow. FedEx pioneered most of this, but Amazon, in particular, is taking it to another level.

When you're able to do that, it changes the game. If I just pulled the last trash bag out of the box in the kitchen, do I want to drive to Target and buy another box of trash bags? Or would I rather get on my computer, hit three keys on Amazon, and know that those trash bags will be here tomorrow? What other businesses are going to be able to do things like that? Same-day repair on your car, or same-day repair on appliances, or same-day delivery of whatever. Everybody wants a different color, or a different shape, or a different size. This high-speed, ubiquitous communication will continue to enable the individualization of products and the productization of certain services.

THE TRANSFORMATIVE POWER OF TECHNOLOGY

With the right technology, you can turn just about any service into something repetitive. Look what Uber and Lyft have done. There are companies doing the same thing with picking up your dog's mess in the yard. With technology, it's just writing applications and plugging them all together. Uber was a technological wonder to a lot of people when it started. It was amazing to ask for a car and by the time you got to your front door, it would be sitting there. And you would know that you were looking for a silver Camry and the driver's name was Johnson. But really, from a technological standpoint, there was nothing there that didn't exist a year before. GPS and apps and all the functionality for them to make that business happen already existed. They are just building blocks that Uber put together in a different configuration to solve the problem.

So, what are they going to do next? I personally think transportation as a service is very viable. I think the trucking industry is going to be drastically disrupted with this concept. Currently if you have one hundred tons of widgets and you want them picked up and taken to Florida, you have to call a broker. The broker finds the truckers and negotiates the rates. But in the near future, you'll use an app and say, "I have one hundred tons of widgets. I want it to go to Orlando," and people will just respond to you the way Uber drivers do. That's going to really disrupt transportation and delivery—and make it more efficient and effective, too.

Technology will continue to evolve. Smartphones are able to monitor a diabetic's glucose levels, as well as monitor heart rate and pulse. There's no limit to the number of things smartphones will be able to do for us going forward that we haven't experienced yet.

We have a partner today that builds mobile apps for maintenance management systems, and customers can literally go to the app store and download them. Too often, software developers design overly complex systems based on server technology and then realize that they've just made something that's unnecessarily complicated—and, more importantly, obsolete. As soon as the next version of whatever comes out, all that connectivity that was customized doesn't work anymore.

It's better to just pull up on your phone what you want to do and then do it—build an emulation of the product you are trying to use as opposed to trying to connect to the product you're trying to use.

Key Takeaways

- Data management systems help you understand what you own, which can save you money.

- Digital capability can help your business respond to a changing environment and improve efficiencies and the customer experience.

- Change is a chance to improve your business model.

- Personal technology and commercial technology are growing similar, meaning that your customers will likely be comfortable with technological changes in the ways you interact with them.

CHAPTER 7

PEOPLE

"I worry that business leaders are more interested in material gain than they are in having the patience to build up a strong organization, and a strong organization starts with caring for their people."

—John Wooden

MANAGING PEOPLE IS a lot like being a coach. You have to understand personality types. You have to know whom to slap on the back and whom to kick in the ass. You have to understand where people's strengths are and play to them. You have to be observant enough to know when people are bored and need more interesting tasks to perform. And you have to understand what motivates them.

Whether you're a manager or a coach, you have to be yourself. You can read about how someone else was a successful coach, someone like the great college basketball coach John Wooden, for instance. No one has come close to his success. But, if you go out on the court and try to be John Wooden, you will fail. You are who you are.

You also have to have integrity. Tell people the truth, whether it's what they want to hear or not. I don't ask people to do things that I wouldn't do alongside them. I also try to show respect for what everyone can bring to the table.

LISTEN TO THE ON-THE-GROUND DOERS—THEY'RE THE REAL EXPERTS

Up until now, reliability has been driven from the top down. The people who are doing the work, the ones with thirty years' experience with their hands on the machines, could do as good, or better, a job at determining reliability of equipment. The craftspeople who actually do the work bring a lot to the table, but unfortunately, they don't have much of a voice. One key component as to why this was the case in the past had to do with the prohibitive cost of computing. Maintenance techs were not given access to technology that would have made them much more capable of predicting maintenance issues. The people at the top of many organizations failed to catch on to this; they kept the computing power at the top, where presumably it would get the most bang for the buck. It was tough to justify handing a five-thousand-dollar machine plus a five-thousand-dollar copy of software to a technician who makes twenty dollars an hour. If you're going to make a ten-thousand-dollar investment, you'll choose to spend it on the few with engineering degrees rather than the many with toolboxes. But when the cost of hardware and software drops, and you add in ubiquitous connectivity, you now have the ability to start at the bottom and work your way up. This trend is flipping the old top-down model on its head.

Thanks to the disruption of silicon economics, you're finally going to get votes from the technicians on the ground. Not only do we have the ability to connect our technicians with tons of computing power, but also the tools in their toolbox are more accurate than they used to be. You're going to get thoughts, ideas, and feedback about maintenance decisions by those engaged in the maintenance itself.

WINNING HEARTS AND MINDS

Respecting that the knowledge the on-the-ground expert has to offer can be an important approach when asking the workforce to embrace a change in process as large as adopting an entire system. Generally, people don't readily embrace change. Workforces are capable of submarining software rollouts. The attitude is, "We don't care; we ain't doing it." In a case like that, you potentially have a million-dollar box of shelfware that no one will use. To be successful, you need to win the hearts and minds of the workforce.

Whenever I train technicians, I always try to find something of value to *them*. How do you identify this value? It's simple: Ask them. "Six months from now, when this system is up and running, what aspect of it will you really love? What will it do to make your life easier?"

Take, for example, airline mechanics. Too often mechanics find themselves trying to diagnose what is wrong with a piece of equipment that gave odd readings to a pilot but seems to be working fine now. Those mechanics would give anything to know who worked on that equipment last. I would teach mechanics how to look up previous work orders on any piece of equipment, thus giving them the ability to call that last mechanic to find out what he did.

Pay attention to what will make the system work for the people who will be using it. You've got to give them something tangible, or they won't have a reason to engage. Every time you discover functionality that meets the needs of the users, make a specific point in your training to show how the software makes their job easier or makes them look smarter. Do that, and people will embrace what they're being asked to take on.

For smaller groups, I try to be a little disarming by asking them about their jobs and what they would change if they could. If they were their boss for a day, what would they change? If they were the CEO of their company for a day, what would they change? I try to capture those ideas so I understand what their heartburn is, where they're frustrated, where they might take an interest, and how to present the technology in a way that they can relate to it. In trying to discover those answers, I find out who are the followers, the dreamers, and the leaders.

It can be tricky to find out what will engage individuals when training a large group of people. It's important to split up the large group into manageable numbers. Start with a training matrix. Define who needs to know what so the training can be targeted. Begin with job descriptions and responsibilities, and then identify the optimal content. A matrix will help ensure that all job groups receive the training they require and will give you the ability to plan training module content.

Once you get into the classroom and begin teaching technology to adults, it matters how you configure the room. When you put ten adults into a room, no one is going to tell you that they don't understand the material. They don't want to look bad in front of their peers. You need to be able to recognize that they are lost. If I'm instructing, I want a long, linear room with an aisle down the middle and trainees in pairs on either side of the aisle. I want to be able to see every screen. I stand at the back instead of the front so I can see that everyone has the right screen up before I move on to the next concept.

AN ORGANIC APPROACH TO TRAINING

Classroom training is great, but it's only so effective. People learn differently—some are auditory learners, some are visual, and some are both. Some people take an online computer-based training session once, and they've got it. Others need help individually for a few days when the system first goes live.

Successful implementations generally provide training immediately before the system goes live, giving people maximum exposure the week before so they don't forget what they've learned. Most companies have a paradigm of using Monday as a day for a fresh start. I'd rather provide training Monday through Wednesday and turn on the new system on a Thursday for continuity within the workweek. I contend that you'll gain a much better retention rate if users can look at the new system today and use it tomorrow without the interruption of a weekend.

Another important dynamic of a successful rollout and adoption involves an organic approach to training. In any group there are going to be one or two individuals who naturally latch on to the new software. The people who get it are your disciples. Day to day, these will be people others on the shift naturally turn to for help and guidance as they ramp up. If you can identify these magnets of instruction, they can be a huge asset in not only developing a trained workforce but also boosting your adoption rate as they lead by example with the new system.

Back in the 1960s, if you owned a copier at your business, it was probably a Xerox copier. Xerox shifted their sales model from selling devices to selling copies, toner, and paper. Xerox would visit the office monthly to clean and fill the copiers. A reading to determine usage was taken and the customer was charged accordingly. After this new revenue model was established, the challenge became how to increase usage. Xerox found that the collective intelligence in using the copier was directly attributable to the skill set of the person who sat closest to it. If you didn't use the copier all the time, you'd walk over, try to make a copy, and then ask the person in the cubical closest to it how it worked. So, Xerox went on a manhunt. They visited every customer and provided free training for the three people closest to each machine. Their revenue spiked as a result. By teaching the folks closest to the machine, they in turn taught everyone else.

What Xerox discovered was that after you think you've rolled out training to the people who make sense on paper, there's some value in going around and just seeing who gets it quickly and who is energized for whatever reason, and then giving them some extra time and attention and visibility.

You can learn a lot from watching how people interact with the technology they already use daily to determine how they'll be most comfortable trying a new system. What apps or tools are they looking at when they're ignoring you? The answer will tell you what tools they are most productive with and how they can be productive using a computer system to do their jobs. Also pay attention to what device people turn to first when they need to answer a question—is it a phone, a PC, or something else? It's interesting to me that so many people of a certain age go straight to a phone. I can call an IT person in my office and say, "Windows is giving me a hard time, and this is the symptom I've got." The IT person won't touch a PC; instead, they'll grab their phone and google whatever I've just said. People who solve problems that way have a tendency, in my view, to be more intuitive and effective. They're trying to learn more about the problem before they give you an answer.

SHOW ME THE MONEY

Nothing, however, is as powerful of an incentive to try something new as money. Do you want to know how your people act? Do you want to know why your people do the things they do? You need to study how you pay them. If you pay them as an hourly employee, guess what? You're going to get hourly employees. If you pay them in some fashion that rewards good quality, then you're going to get good quality. It's compensation that drives the habit.

I've had twenty different pay plans and projects over the years. Near the beginning, we had a whiteboard in our office showing the growing balance of money in our company bank account for the month. Employees got a percentage of those deposits each month, which made up the bulk of their salary. I was trying to make sure that everybody, regardless of their function, understood that putting money in the bank was the name of the game. It drove some really good behavior. I had employees on Friday afternoons taking the initiative to drive out to customer sites to pick up a check and take it to the bank themselves, because they knew that that would increase their paycheck for the following month. Now we have a bonus plan based on recurring revenue.

You have to remember that people go to work to make money. If you're paying them to work, you need to incentivize them so they'll give you the correct outcomes. What do you want to see as a result of this effort? Pay them to change. Pay them for outcomes.

FINDING NATURAL LEADERS AND HIDDEN TALENT

People are different at work than they are outside of work. When I first meet with a group of people around a technology project, I try to read people both in the environment and outside of it. I try to get as many people as possible out for a beer or whatever means of socializing fits their culture after the first meeting or two, just to see who they really are.

Seeing how people behave outside of work also tells me a little bit about the work environment, because people behave at work based on how they're managed or how their company culture works. Some companies are very conservative and treat mistakes as a problem; there might even be reprimands or punishments. I tend to go the complete opposite direction. I find, generally speaking, that people making mistakes are trying to do something interesting, and that's a positive thing.

Everyone reacts to stress or big changes differently. Whether they are worried about job security or positioning themselves for a promotion, people will act differently given the circumstance and their personality. Some are fight-or-flight, while others are heads down. The more opportunities I create to get to know people, the better I understand how they'll react to the change a new system will bring.

> **The more opportunities I create to get to know people, the better I understand how they'll react to the change a new system will bring.**

You're always looking for leadership, right? If you have ten brand-new Marines, you want to know which one is going to be the platoon leader. You're always looking for who's going to stand out and provide a little leadership or thought. Differentiating those people early on is important.

I think company leaders may underestimate how tech-savvy some of their people are, especially if they come from an older demographic that didn't grow up around technology. It's never good to underestimate what kind of skill sets you might have in the room. When people are not at work, their hobbies take them in all sorts of directions. And you'd be amazed how a guy who likes to build model remote-controlled electric cars can translate that skill into robotics. If you're replacing some menial tasks on an assembly line with a robot, you've found the guy to program and operate the robot. A number of people love to play games online. Online gaming is an amazing teaching tool for hand-eye coordination and analytical cause-and-effect processes.

To learn what people do away from the job, create opportunities to interact in a relaxed atmosphere. Foster break environments that are comfortable and not necessarily within the fishbowl of the company but where leaders and workers can mingle. Make time for group lunches, providing food and giving people the opportunity to just interact. Whenever I get my people together, I try to move from table to table. I ask them what they're doing this weekend, or what they do after work. My line is, "What are you up to when you're not a welder/plumber/etc.?" I just try to get them to talk about themselves.

A lot of people who aren't comfortable talking about themselves are very comfortable talking about their kids. I was talking with a forklift driver at one plant. We discussed maintenance at the plant in general, and he shared his frustrations with machinery that wouldn't work properly, how the maintenance department wasn't very efficient in taking care of preventative maintenance, and how they were even less efficient when it came to handling repairs and breakdowns. I got to know the guy fairly well over the course of a few days. It turns out that he was the state director for a soccer league that involved thousands of kids, and he was one of the most prolific Excel spreadsheet users I'd ever met, yet he never touched a PC at work. This forklift driver knew more about pivot tables than some engineers, and he learned it managing ten thousand girls playing soccer.

Another way to have company leaders learn the skills hidden among their employees is to get groups that don't normally interact during the workday involved in something together outside of work. Find a way to cross-pollinate those people in something that brings them together, whatever that something might be. We sponsor a grade school a few blocks from our office, and we've adopted a first-grade classroom. Once a month, a group of six or eight Projetech employees go to the classroom and bring a learning project. Sometimes it's mixing paint colors and teaching the kids how to make green from blue and yellow, while other times we make soda overflow a bottle by dropping in some Mentos. Regardless of the project, volunteering at the school together gets people from different areas of the business working together on a common objective. It helps them find out what managers and production workers or different departments have in common. It opens up lines of communication as well.

Go out of your way to spend time with people you don't know. When we go to conferences, I take ten employees with me, and I expect them to split up—no more than one person from Projetech at every table in the room—so each of them gets to know someone new. You've got to get out of your comfort zone, and you've got to go meet somebody. Let's say you walk into a seminar, and there's a row with five empty chairs. Human nature is that you're going to sit in the middle chair. But if you really want to learn something, you've got to sit down next to somebody.

CULTIVATING LIFELONG LEARNERS

Whenever we begin any career, we're taught a certain way of doing things. The first job I had as a mechanic, someone taught me how to thread a piece of pipe and hang a piece of duct work, explaining, "This is the way it should be done." For me to go back and re-evaluate that teaching from a different perspective decades later feels kind of blasphemous. How can I question those tenets? It's hard to challenge the things you've learned as you grow older.

I took a class offered by Xavier University that talked about how adults learn. What I took away from the class was that when you're young, you're a sponge. When you're young, you want to learn. And when you're young, you want to try things. But twelve or sixteen years of formal education works that natural curiosity out of you.

If you sit a youngster down in front of a PC and say, "This is a mouse—point and click," the kid will start pointing and clicking. Children, because of their natural curiosity, will simply execute and then learn from it. Adults with no computer expertise or exposure will point and then say, "Well, what happens when I click it?" They want to know the outcome before they execute because adults want to know the answers before they pull the trigger.

Education is very important. Some companies are supportive of education. They reimburse tuition for employees going to night school or taking online classes. They set time aside during the day for people to sit and learn skills around technology. On the other hand, other companies will hire a plumber and never give him a plumbing class again the rest of his life just because he walked in the door as a plumber.

It's a mistake. The companies that embrace continuous education, lifelong learning, are the ones that get ahead. "Lunch and learn" is a great concept. If you feed somebody, you have their attention, so take advantage of that and nourish their mind for thirty to forty minutes as well.

When companies hire, they need to look for attitude and aptitude. I think almost any job skill can be taught. In our company, we can teach anyone how to use Maximo or work with spreadsheets. We look for the right people, then train them on the right skill sets. Someone may have twenty years of experience, but is he the right fit for our culture? Is he growing?

THE NONTRADITIONAL ROUTE

How people learn is indicative of what they may or may not be good at. People who are content with the status quo are not typically going to be the contributors. When you're looking for somebody to help you drive a project, you need somebody who wants to learn.

We have several examples of nontraditional hires at Projetech. We had a math teacher interview for a training position, and it was clear to everyone that he was very bright. We steered him toward our programmers—he fit in with the team and turned out to be one of the better programmers I've ever known. I once hired a waiter because he had good customer skills, and he turned out to be a pretty good customer support person. My CIO has a degree in accounting and finance, and he's also the chief technology officer of the company. My controller, my finance guy, has a degree in computer science. The finance guy's the technical guy, and the technical guy's the finance guy.

Our people have very high standards and expect certain things, and sometimes we have to remember to keep our minds open when hiring. I had a conversation with a few of my managers not too long ago because an open job position stated specifically that the candidate had to have a bachelor's degree. Three of the five people in the room didn't have bachelor's degrees. I said, "Why are the three of you being excluded from applying for this job? I get that you want people with formal education, but why do they have to have a bachelor's degree in computer science? None of you do."

AVOID FEAR OF LOSING JOBS

A good system is going to create opportunity. There will be people who at first will be concerned about job security whenever a process is digitized. But as you collect better data, and as your systems mature, there will be a need for additional people to analyze data and make good decisions around that data. People who have a role in planning will also be valuable. And this is a skill set that many of the people worrying about the system displacing their jobs would be very qualified for, either from the outset or with a little training, because of their understanding of the process or the vertical market that they're in.

Companies can frame the change in a way that emphasizes opportunity. Technology does create opportunity. Give the message that this change creates new jobs, and encourage employees to consider how they might be a good fit for one of those jobs or what kind of training might be required to find their fit. Being trained on technology might enable someone to go to the next grade level, or three grade levels above that. Or it might be their way into management, if that's what they aspire to do. Present it all from a transitional perspective and emphasize the positive. Everybody knows what the downside is, but it's not something that you dwell on. Make certain that's not the last thing employees hear when they leave the room.

With the proliferation of cloud-based applications, the number of information technology professionals needed hasn't changed, but the skill sets have changed. People need to be more collaborative, communicative, and security-minded. They may now be in a position of quality assurance as they manage an important service-level agreement with a vendor, making decisions about bandwidth, licenses, security products, encryption, and the degree of latency the group accepts.

Don't count out any group as unable to learn. Instead, match people with those who can help them upgrade their skills quickly. I worked with a metal recycling company that had a workforce with basic skills, since most were involved with moving scrap from a truck to a conveyor, or similar tasks. They figured out who in their workforce had at least used a computer or a keyboard, or had a smartphone, and they teamed them up with a partner who might not be as literate in that skill. They used a similar approach to help those who weren't native English speakers learn the terms needed to do the work. By working in pairs, the collective intelligence of the workforce went up faster.

I use a similar approach when I train groups and find people who are very uncomfortable with technology. I know who is keeping up since I always place myself where I can see the trainees' computer screens. If someone doesn't reach out to a coworker on their own to get help, I'll make a new seating chart for the next class so that those who are learning quickly are paired with those who need more help, thus bringing them along without singling them out.

MANAGEMENT IN TRANSITION

Much of the workforce today is maturing, and that's resulted in a few trends. When someone is near the end of their career, they often are less inclined to be risk takers. Also, they sometimes are less engaged with their peers. The company then runs the risk of losing a tremendous amount of knowledge when that person retires.

You don't want it to be a surprise when a very experienced person walks in and says they're retiring. You need to have a plan. And making sure that everybody has a mentor inside of your businesses is the best way for that knowledge to be passed along.

Mentorship is huge. People learn from people. If you don't have a mentor, go find one. And if you're a company that doesn't encourage mentorship, consider changing this. Mentors and mentees don't have to be within the same department or skill set. Engineers can talk to production people and vice versa—you cross-pollinate information throughout the business that way. If you sit with someone who does something different than you, for even a few days or a week, you get an appreciation for what their job is. And oftentimes that parallels back to either something that you directly control or something you need to understand why you're doing because of the way it impacts somebody else.

The competitive nature of businesses is forcing companies to do things they may have been hesitant to embrace in the past. There's the actuarial table that's working against the older worker being supplanted by the younger worker, or the person who grew up with technology versus the person who had to adopt it in their forties. But I think companies face the same thing. Some have been able to be competitive or at least survive without embracing change. But as those companies mature, they either have to join in, or they're going to get passed up. In particular, this is a challenge for small businesses.

Take the sixty-year-old CEO who started with one truck for wiring houses when he was twenty-eight years old but now has a team of ninety guys in vehicles doing new construction and renovation and repairs all over the city. They're successful, but they've never invested in technology. It's a very difficult exit strategy for that CEO. On the other hand, when the guy who has embraced technology all along is trying to sell his business, he can show that the books are in order and the dispatch system makes sense. The history on all of his customers is available, as is the way they handle work and processes and the training programs they've put in place. Those companies are very marketable companies, and they'll live on as opposed to just being harvested and fading off into the sunset.

If you've only got five years until you want to sell your business, you need to start right now. Have a meeting and put together a prioritized list of five things that you need to do—because you can only do one or two things well at a time. Start working on the first things right away. There's always low-hanging fruit; there's always little opportunities that have big returns. And once you start those changes in your business, the next change is easier than the previous one. You can't do everything, but you can do something.

Key Takeaways

- Understand your employees' personalities to manage your team well.

- The on-the-ground doers have a lot to teach you, especially with regards to technology.

- Respecting people helps them embrace change. Recognize what is important to them.

- Training doesn't end in the classroom; it keeps going after systems go "live" and people begin to use the system.

- Look for and nurture natural leaders and hidden talent in your organization.

- Be a lifelong learner and encourage others to do the same.

- Encourage mentorship to develop people and keep institutional knowledge from walking out the door with retirees.

CHAPTER 8

STAYING SAFE
AND SMART

"Adversity is the state in which man most easily becomes
acquainted with himself, being especially free of admirers then."

—John Wooden

THERE IS SO much that can be done technologically today, but companies need to pause and think each time there is an opportunity to adopt something new. Many pieces of equipment today are being built with intelligence or with communications capabilities. But should you plug in that equipment just because you can?

SMART UPGRADES

Go back to the most important principle, which is to begin with the end in mind. Is this something that needs to be tracked or are you tracking thousands of data points that have absolutely no impact on your processes or your throughput or your reliability? Pallets are a great example. Walmart tracks pallets because it's important to know where they are. Other companies may have pallets, too, but tracking them has little impact on their success and therefore isn't worth the effort.

> ### Begin with the end in mind.

The second consideration is whether the organization is prepared to handle communicating with that asset. Many manufacturing environments and a lot of remote locations do not have the ability to communicate that data. They don't have Wi-Fi, they don't have a network, and they don't have the telecommunications infrastructure needed to take that data and send it back to the local office. Right now, in 2023, 5G has the promise to change manufacturing in some peoples' minds. But some caution that the problem with 5G is that 24 percent of the plant floors in the United States don't have any Wi-Fi.[1] The cost of adding this technology to the plant floor is very high, and there needs to be some tangible potential payback for it before people are going to use it. So, you can put 5G-capable components on all these factory floors, but there's nothing for them to talk to. I think you'll find technology like 5G is going to be more prevalent in Greenfield applications than in retrofitting the legacy manufacturing environment.

It's back to the ROI. What are you going to get out of it? But as you are making that determination, keep an eye on when advances may make your current technology obsolete—your business case for upgrading technology can be forced upon you. Everyone doesn't have to be an early adopter, but companies should stay aware enough of advancements in technology to be open to the potential technology could bring you. Don't be so locked into the way you do things that you miss the chance to be creative, and don't dismiss it so much that you get left behind because technology has moved on without you.

THE EVOLUTION OF AGRICULTURE

I don't think farmers have ever been considered the bleeding edge or out in front for anything. But over the last twenty-five years, they have embraced GPS, mapping technologies, and weather information, and they have become pretty sophisticated at what they do. By using technology to increase their yields, there is at least some data out there about what the average farmer can get in yield per acre today versus twenty or twenty-five years ago.[2] And that data is almost all technologically driven, either through the equipment they use or through the techniques that they employ. This isn't a wave change; it's evolved over time—a generational change. Third-generational farmers all have cell phones by now. Thirty-five years ago, you had to wait for Dad to come back from the field to be able to tell him something. Today, you can call him on the phone. But this didn't happen overnight; it was a more natural change. Instead of "I have to go get this technology," it's "I have it. I'm familiar with it. I know what to do with it. Now I can apply it."

The same thing can be done by maintenance and reliability professions by paying attention to what they have or what they're using naturally, or what their mechanics have on their person. Go where your technology comfort takes you as opposed to trying to force yourself so far out that it doesn't make sense.

STAYING SECURE

We can connect all of our assets, but we have to know how we will track and secure those connected assets. If you use a cellular network, anybody on-site with a phone could manipulate, hack, or steal that data. When you use different protocols, whether you're using Bluetooth, Wi-Fi, or your own network, you're connecting all that data to something. What's the control? Who's in charge of it?

The first question people ask when you talk to them about taking their systems off-site is security. The proliferation of sophisticated manners for hacking systems means that security is at the forefront of everyone's minds. The old model was that you built a fortress with a big, fat, thick wall, you put all your goodies inside the fortress, and you just made sure that nobody breached the wall. You can't manage it that way anymore because there are too many remote outposts. It's not all in the castle anymore. This issue escalated between 2020 and 2022, when so many people worked from home. How are you securing work from home conversations and data transfers? As workforces diverge, it's harder to keep things safe and secure.

The most serious problem companies had twenty years ago was people downloading data onto a thumb drive. It's still the number one problem. That's how data gets out the door. The second problem is sticky note passwords on monitors. That stuff hasn't changed a whole lot. What has changed is the explosion in the number of places that can be breached, because we have so many remote work sites and so many more systems today. It's great to connect everybody's phone to the corporate email, but then everybody's phone is a potential hack. What happens if a phone is lost? What happens when the employee leaves the company? What happens if that employee tries to download the price list or the engineering drawings and then leaves the company or tries to sell that information?

When you were looking for data space years ago, you were buying ping, pipe, and power: connectivity to the internet, the size of the connection to the internet, and electricity. You wanted to make sure that your internet connectivity was redundant, that your power and air-conditioning systems were redundant. Those were the criteria as you bought data space. Back then, it was how much a foot, or how much a box, or how much a rack cost, and that's what you paid for.

I think that's probably way down the list now that you're going to put your system somewhere else. Today, you're asking, "What sort of security certifications do they have? Who has physical access to control to this site? What security products are present?" You have the idea of a firewall that won't let the bad guys in. Well, there is a box, or what looks like a computer—that is a physical firewall. A lot of firewalls have gone soft today. They have to, because sometimes the nefarious code is arriving at companies already embedded in a software product.

A number of communication companies have software-defined security, and it's part of the communication pipe. In that fiber, they are watching the packets as they roll down the line at lightning speed, but they're monitoring for the out-of-place packet, the bad guy. Data inspection at the edge is a great way to protect the organizational whole.

There are so many sophisticated ways to manage and maintain secure environments today. We get security interview documents, and there are pages and pages of questions asking, "How do you do this?" and "How do you do that?" "Do you transmit your data encrypted when you store or archive your data? Is it at rest? Is it encrypted? What would it cost to do that?" Sometimes the most extensive security just doesn't make economic sense.

That security cost needs to be considered before a company increases connectivity. I've got ubiquitous bandwidth; I've got an ethernet cable here plugged into my PC; I've got Wi-Fi here at the house—two different versions: 2.6 and 5.0. There's a cell phone here, so I just knocked out four ways that I can connect or communicate.

There are also four highways that need to be monitored and managed from a security perspective. They're all different, and they're all important. The more diverse and the more decentralized the workforce becomes, the harder it is to lock it down. It's an exponential growth in devices, time, and communication methodologies.

We all have phones, we all have computers—some of us have multiple phones and computers—we have smart TVs, we have routers. With all the equipment in my house, there's probably fifteen or twenty electronic signals. Some of them are Wi-Fi-enabled, some of them are hardwired, some of them use cell signals, some of them don't do anything. But they're all vulnerabilities.

The important thing about buying a software product is that after you outlay the capital, you need to manage and maintain it. So many companies are vulnerable today because they're running older products. Most software products have numbering systems that track different versions. Well, when you get more than one or two versions behind, that software provider often no longer supports security for that age of product.

You can have everything in the world locked down, but the software that you're running is in itself vulnerable because of its age. And more than likely, that's happened because somebody bought it, but they didn't budget the money to manage and maintain it. Upgrade cycles are expensive—that's how companies get behind.

Our philosophy is that you have to keep current. There are a lot of reasons for that. There's risk in aging products; there's risk in losing your most knowledgeable employees. If you outsource it, typically they've got a team of people who keep things current for you.

Imagine that a power supply company decides to construct a new clean coal technology power plant. In order to bring the plant online, the company will spend five or six billion dollars, work for a decade, and employ a crew of thousands. There's a lot of hype around building the new plant; however, after the ribbon-cutting, the real work of the plant begins. In a similar way, you will find that the work of bringing a system online can be a massive undertaking, and the excitement tends to be front-loaded. Yet the real work of managing systems begins after you go live. A system needs constant attention by way of day-to-day system management and support in order to maintain peak performance. A lot of companies underestimate or even ignore the fact that they should be concerned with these ongoing system administration responsibilities.

BE PREPARED FOR BUSINESS INTERRUPTION

Sometimes when companies automate systems, they forget about how things worked before the systems were employed. When a company is operating everything electronically and then loses a fiber connection and loses power, can they still do their job? Can they get anything done with the loss of this new technology? What happens when something changes?

We had a client with an oil refinery in Galveston, Texas. The oil tanker would come in and remain in the Gulf. The company would pump oil from the tanker to the refinery and make gasoline, jet fuel, and so on. When Hurricane Ike came through their region and they had to get the tankers out of there, they had to shut the refinery down.

That refinery had been making fuel for decades uninterrupted. When it came time to turn everything back on, there was no process or procedure for that. Engineers had to go to retirement communities and pull guys out of bingo games and sit them down in front of blueprints and say, "If we open this valve before we open that valve, what might happen?" They finally did get everything up and running again, and they made sure to document that process and procedure so they would have it should something like that ever happen again.

DIGITAL DATA LEADS TO BETTER HURRICANE RESPONSE

A small city in southwest Florida provides its citizens with water reuse, wastewater, and stormwater services. Unfortunately, their service area is prone to hurricanes each year, which means they need reliable ways to restore service to their customers—and fast.

At the time of its implementation, no utility company had tried a cloud-based maintenance management system. But the region needed a better method than a paper-based system to gather, manage, and store the critical operational data they used to make decisions when responding to hurricanes. They also lacked a robust solution for storing this information securely but in a way that could be easily accessed during emergency situations.

With the move to a digital maintenance management system, the city can access crucial data regardless of the weather. Integration of real-time meter values into the system helps the city be proactive and make informed decisions while keeping problems caused by

continued

storms from getting worse. Since digital systems are scalable and can address any asset, they can easily expand to include production wells, lift stations, and other vital assets. Management found that the robust reporting tools helped them demonstrate the flow of expenditures and validate budget requirements.

NOT BUSINESS AS USUAL

Business interruption is no joke, and it can happen any number of ways. Another example is what happened to JetBlue. They were one of the first airlines to use a Voice over Internet Protocol (VOIP) telephone system. Their reservationists worked remotely and connected to the company's seat inventory, flights, and so on, through phones on their desks that were run over internet protocol. The system worked very well; it was extremely efficient, able to run hundreds of aircraft and manage dozens of reservationists. At least until there was a blizzard that shut down all of their operations in New York City, which is where they were based.

When the outage the blizzard caused was over seventy-two hours later, JetBlue tried to get their planes back in the air. The entire system was brought to its knees because it couldn't handle the volume of reloading everything at once. There were too many calls being made, too many people trying to change their reservations and get to where they wanted to go. Their VOIP system was being choked to the point where JetBlue employees couldn't communicate internally. They just didn't have the bandwidth to get it done.

At LaGuardia, there were flight crews in one room and operations people on the other side of the wall, and they couldn't communicate with one another because they had embraced this new technology to a fault. Even though they were physically sitting next to one another, the airline came to a halt because they couldn't call one another on the phone.

Another problem that may be lying in wait for companies is their disaster recovery system. Many companies have one in place, but few test it. Businesspeople will claim that they have backed up their systems. That provides a nice warm and fuzzy feeling that there is a solution in place in case of a problem, but I would venture to say that the majority, if not the vast majority, of people have never really tested the backup as their sole option for coming back online to make sure that it actually works.

We all know friends who have used iCloud for years to back up the photos they take on their phone. They hit a button on their iPhone and say, "See, all my pictures are here in the cloud; I don't have to worry about it." And then one day they drop their phone in the toilet and find out that the iCloud connection was never made because no one ever checked it to see if it was working.

On another level, businesses do exactly the same thing. They'll call a meeting and say, "This is our disaster plan. This is how we'll do it." Often these meetings happen as a result of a recent disaster. After all, most of us don't plan for a disaster. Usually what happens is that a disaster occurs, and then we do a postmortem on it. We ask, "What did we learn? What should we do differently next time? What's the plan if this happens again?" Then we come up with a plan, document it, and put it on the shelf. Nobody touches it again, and we don't try it out to see if it works.

This is something we have to do in our business; it's part of being a service provider. We have to take a backup of a system and rebuild that system from zero every so many months to prove that our systems are working appropriately. Not just once, but several times a year. But most companies don't do that.

EYES ON THE GOAL

Too often businesses only look backward at what they don't want to repeat again as opposed to looking forward. Instead, when we're doing something new, as we're putting the plans in place, we should pause for a minute and think what we will do with this new thing in the case of a disaster.

Some groups have multiple fiber feeds from different providers to their data centers. They feel secure because they have redundancy, but nobody has ever walked outside and cut the cable to see if the backup provider's service can do the job. They think they've done enough by providing the redundancy. We worked with a data center in Indianapolis. They had dual power feeds. In fact, they had the luxury of having two electrical companies within so many thousand feet of their facility. The whole place was built around this redundant electricity, but they never cross-wired it correctly inside the building. The day came that one of those electrical feeds went down, and it caused half of their building to lose power. All because nobody checked it, so no one knew that it wasn't wired correctly.

Many years ago, hospitals were required to have emergency generators. In case the power went off in the hospital, the generator would kick on and life-supporting equipment would have power. Hospitals spent millions of dollars on diesel generators. But they discovered that, if they didn't test their generators every month, a lot of times the generators wouldn't run when the hospital needed them to. And the hospitals couldn't just leave their diesel tanks untouched. If you put one thousand gallons of diesel fuel in a tank and forget about it, it will stratify into layers of water and goo and won't be worth anything. The tanks have to be dipped and flushed and changed every so often. Nobody thought about these things ahead of time, so they found out about them the hard way when there was an emergency and the generators didn't work.

It's not enough to have a disaster plan and walk away from it. You have to maintain your disaster plan. You can't make untested redundancy your only solution, either, or it will just give you a false sense of security.

Looking ahead is even more important if you are on the leading edge of new technology. A great example of such a mistake was the Astrodome. It was the largest enclosed building in the world at the time. When it first opened, technicians didn't have the humidity under control. The air-conditioning could treat the air, but because there weren't any air movers to circulate the air, the air would get trapped up against the ceiling. The air would get too warm and then stratify, making it literally rain inside the Astrodome. People sitting around the outfield would suddenly get caught in an indoor down-pour. There were no rain checks, either. People learned to bring umbrellas, or an usher would hand out pieces of plastic to use as protection.[3]

This all happened because the air-conditioning was designed more for comfort at the seating level, and no one had anticipated the fact that this layer of warm air was just sitting under the top of the dome without any attention. It was a volume problem. They knew how many cubic feet of air they needed to treat. But no one accounted for getting the air off the ceiling down to the HVAC equipment so it could be treated.

What we can learn from rain inside the Astrodome is that whether you build the biggest building in the world or the biggest data center or create a brand-new operating system or release brand-new code, there will be the unknown to deal with. Be prepared for that by finding a way to give yourself some type of soft opening of sorts so you can deal with it before too many people are affected.

 ## *Key Takeaways*

- Upgrade wisely—make sure your system is ready for the upgrade, but don't let technology move on without you.
- New technology requires new security measures.
- Proactively think about the potential for business interruption and test disaster recovery plans.

CHAPTER 9

WHAT'S ON THE
HORIZON

"It's the little things that are vital.
Little things make big things happen."

—John Wooden

IN HIS BOOK *Business @ the Speed of Thought,*[1] Bill Gates talks about the tendency in the technology field to promise a certain deliverable on a certain timeline, which is usually missed. But when it's finally ready, the deliverable often is exponentially better. We have to be willing to miss the mark sometimes and, when we know we have something amazing, give ourselves time to find the moment where the business case makes sense. Sometimes that takes some discovery. Sometimes it just takes waiting for the world to catch up to you. In those cases, you might have to put it on the shelf and let it come to you when the time is right—and that's not easy to manage. Companies face expectations from shareholders or investors. Overexuberant executives make pie-in-the-sky predictions about when their latest technology will be available and what it can do that no one believes they can meet—you can almost picture the company's engineers squirming around in their chairs.

So, I'm not going to predict how soon these things on the horizon may arrive. But I do see some possibilities I'd like to share.

> **Technology always evolves, and reliability can be improved as technology evolves. Like you, I'm excited to see what's coming next.**

SYSTEMS EVOLVE WITH MOBILITY ADVANCES

Mobility opens up everything. It is far beyond two people having a conversation; it is about the connectivity of assets. Suddenly, we have all this *smart stuff* around us. Instead of being impressed that everything is connected, we should *expect* it. I *expect* that my dishwasher is connected. I *expect* that airplanes are connected. I *expect* that a windmill out in the middle of nowhere in Wyoming is sending out a signal saying, "I'm turning at 38 rpm, and I'm generating 4 megawatts of power." No one lives near that windmill. It's a remote, desolate asset. We take for granted that we can have that type of connectivity to our assets. They should be able to help us make decisions—and even make decisions for us.

The ramifications are staggering. It's Moore's Law in action: The capabilities of digital electronics (processing speed, memory capacity, etc.) will double every two years.[2] He described this law in 1965, and we're now in the second decade of the twenty-first century. Moore was spot on with his prediction, but he did not describe another critical component to the curve: cost. While computers have become smarter and smaller, they've also become cheaper, nearly at the same rate. Add that all together, and you've got the ingredients for a connected planet.

While most people know about Moore's Law, not as many know about Metcalfe's Law, and it's arguably more important. Metcalfe stated that a network's value is proportional to the number of nodes on the network. For example, if a network has ten nodes, its value is one hundred ($10 \times 10 = 100$).[3] So, when you applied this to the ethernet, the speed and openness of the protocol allowed you to connect more devices and thus raise the value and amount of information exchanged. We connected every PC, and hence the proliferation of email, changing business forever.

In 1980, Metcalfe was referring to telephony; they didn't even have the ethernet yet. He was *anticipating* connected devices. Metcalfe's idea was that the more nodes connect, the more information exchange is possible, and the value, or utility, of the data increases. Apply that idea to mobile devices and connected assets, and you can see that the implications are bigger than anybody has fully realized yet. It means that we're right in the middle of a major transformation, an enormous shift, and mobility is at the heart of it.

Enterprise asset management (EAM) is evolving with technology. But in the maintenance management system provider space, there's not a clear choice as to which mobile application a company should choose. With no clear dominant option, there has been a proliferation of dozens of management maintenance system mobile apps, few of which stand out for quality. Once a few key players develop the mobile app that is the top choice for most customers, it will be much easier for SaaS providers to help them make the most of systems on a mobile platform.

CONTINUED NEED TO COORDINATE SYSTEMS ACROSS COMPANY (PC) AND PERSONAL (IOS) DEVICES

Now that technology is ubiquitous, companies have a new problem: They don't have to worry about getting mobile technology into the hands of their employees. Instead, they have to deal with the fact that their employees have already gone mobile, and most likely have multiple devices at their desks or on their person, also known as shadow IT. More than likely, they have a smartphone, and chances are, they like to check email on their iPad. They are bringing their own device to work and have added it to their toolbox. The fact of the matter is that most of any company's employees are walking around with a very smartphone in their pocket that has tons of capabilities.

Gartner describes the phenomenon like this: "Bring your own device, or BYOD, is a disruptive phenomenon where employees bring non-company IT into the organization and demand to be connected to everything—without proper accountability or oversight."[4] All the standard IT concerns apply to these devices: governance, compliance, access control, security. Except with BYOD, the company doesn't own the devices. These companies need to keep in mind that their staff is only going to become more and more connected as time goes on. In a foreseeable future, technology will be embedded on their person, and just by virtue of showing up to work, they will be connected.

Not everything that employees jump into will work out. Remember Google Glass? But don't completely count out the things that fall flat on the first try. For example, look at virtual reality. That was a big thing four years ago. It was going to change the world. It didn't, but now there are some pretty cool virtual reality applications that are practical and worthwhile, as well as fun, such as training. You can immerse someone in a virtual cockpit and teach them to fly a plane and how to react to different situations. In the maintenance reliability industry, virtual reality could help with learning safety procedures and how to perform certain tasks.

Keep an eye on new developments as they come around. Not that you need to jump on them—you don't need to suddenly say, "We're all going to wear Google Glasses as we drive our forklifts"—but you never know what's going to come back around and actually have real application. So, it's a good idea to become a little familiar with new technology. That way, things don't feel so foreign when they're finally practical.

Keep an eye on what people around you are doing, especially younger people. We hire younger people at Projetech because younger people embrace stuff faster. Actually, they're mostly the developers of new technology. They can quickly tell you what is good and bad about the latest thing, giving you just enough information to know the basics and not be intimidated by that technology should it come time to seriously consider it a few years later.

While it requires managing, BYOD does open up myriad possibilities, and if companies embrace the phenomenon, they can quickly discover how valuable connected employees really are. Historically, a lot of companies said, "We have to mobilize our workforce, but how are we going to do it?" For years it was too expensive. Before connectivity was ubiquitous, building infrastructure was massively expensive, and progress was slow. In some ways, companies became paralyzed by the decisions: Do we Wi-Fi every floor? Do we use cellular service? Do we buy Motorola Windows phones or iPhones? The conversation stagnated. Meanwhile, the problem solved itself. If you don't provide your technician with a smartphone, he's going to go out and buy one himself. Companies have been sitting around the conference table arguing about what devices to buy and how to support them, and guess what? Their workforce has gone mobile on its own initiative. It's upside down and backward.

This leaves companies in the position of figuring out how to control BYOD. The hardware, the platforms, the connectivity options are all in place. In fact, if I hired a mechanic today and he didn't have some kind of basic connectivity, I would think that something was wrong. The problem today is managing what he brings with him and providing ways for him to use his device with our systems safely and securely. It's managing the fact that everything's connected, not how to connect it.

UBIQUITOUS CONNECTIVITY

It's not just that technology is everywhere; now we also have the ability to connect from almost anywhere with any device. The faster it gets, the more we can transmit. There wasn't a thought before of taking a two-minute video and sending it to the manufacturer and saying, "This is what I'm looking at with your part." Or "This is the way your machine is operating—what's the deal?" There's a lot of that going on, but it's a tremendous amount of data. It struggles and chokes a lot of cellular networks today.

This affects even companies with limited fiber in their facilities. Visual communication is a massive change, and people communicating in that vein need to be able to express themselves and better articulate the challenges and solutions via video and/or photography. We see this happening in real time on smartphones now, whether you're sharing it in Germany, Asia, or somewhere in between.

The world is simply always connected. There's always a signal somewhere. That leads to powerful communications. Consider the notice on your phone that there's a tornado in the area or there's a child missing whom you can be on the lookout for.

That's connectivity. That's human connectivity. And there's value in that.

SPEED AND LATENCY

Certain applications will not work if the transmission speed is slow. The popular conversation today is edge computing and being able to do all this computing closer to the end point. Information, typically, has been managed the same way. It goes into a data center somewhere and then back out. But what we're starting to see is that at the edge, the end point, of this network connection, they're putting more power, more computing, more security, which is all about speed and allowing users to react faster. The easy example of this is self-driving cars. They don't have seconds to make a decision; they have milliseconds. So that computer has to be very close by, and the latency between the car and the central control on what information is processed and what it should do or how it should react is much closer there.

There's a new term called the MPN, or mobile private network. Currently 5G is the fastest wireless you can have, but the big three—Verizon, AT&T, and T-Mobile—are building these private mobile networks. When a factory floor doesn't have Wi-Fi, or connectivity, companies must look at the cost of cabling it or installing repeaters for traditional cell or Wi-Fi service.

The big players are now offering mobile private networks instead, which means that inside of this campus or building or facility, there is a private network that's wireless and mobile. Any device can connect and utilize it, but all devices on that network are controlled by the privacy of that network. It's specifically for this particular manufacturing facility, so only things the company wants in that network are allowed to be networked. This gives them a lot more control versus open Wi-Fi, where people could be doing whatever.

The idea of communications being ultrafast, with super low latency in terms of reactions and speed time, and private provides a lot of capabilities around what you might want to do. The paranoid people have resisted turning some of their systems loose on what I would call public networks, for fear of intellectual property loss or security. But deploying a mobile private network really opens up a host of opportunities for businesses to take a leap forward in the utilization of technology.

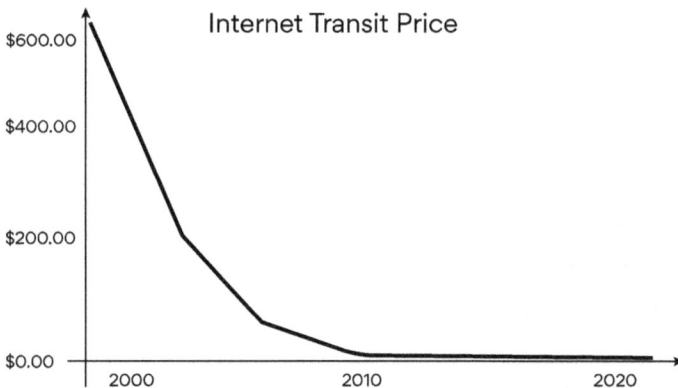

Internet Transit Price

SIMPLIFICATION IN MANUFACTURING

I think there's going to be a massive move in manufacturing toward simplification. If you're making an aircraft engine, when you start talking about 3D printing, digital twins, and virtualization, you can make one part that replaces fifty or 150 other parts. Simplifying the process not only saves time and money—it also enables the speed with which it can change. If you make a new part and it replaces fifty other parts, that's a great thing. But tomorrow, some modification needs to happen. Being able to do that sort of stuff on the fly and make those changes quickly is going to really separate the successful from the not so successful. The people who adapt are going to be better off.

For a few decades, one of the big economic challenges our country has faced is that we've sent a lot of manufacturing offshore. There are reasons for that—labor was cheaper, for one thing. But the recent pandemic impacted our ability to get products from those overseas facilities in a number of ways. People talk about supply chain issues today like they talk about coffee. Everyone knows what it is now. Everyone understands that "supply chain disruption" means "I can't get my stuff."

Manufacturing has gone from the infancy of automation to almost a zenith in that we don't really need people to put things together anymore. Consider how robots are being used more and more in manufacturing. With that automation, labor cost advantages overseas have gone away. I think we're going to see more manufacturing coming back onshore. We're starting to see chip companies like Intel and Nvidia talk about building fab plants, and battery companies talking about building gigafactories in the United States. All this automated manufacturing is going to have an impact on reliability and usability.

When you look at computerized maintenance management, you can see a similar trend. Devices will be self-diagnostic and often self-healing. They're going to be able to say, "Hey, I'm broken; come fix me," or "Hey, I'm broken; I'm going offline for three minutes so that I can fix myself."

There's a dramatic change afoot in terms of where manufacturing is performed and how it's being done. But automation doesn't mean do away with people. There's absolutely a need for people. We're eliminating mundane, repetitive, and dangerous work and putting people in charge of the automation, lifting them up, giving them more responsibility. No one wants to sit on a stool and examine aerosol cans as they go by on a magnetic belt (which, by the way, I did when I was in college). Now there are optical readers that can identify the bad cans and kick them off the line. It's about giving them a higher caliber of work to do. We're eliminating repetitive, boring things and giving people the interesting and creative outlets that all human beings want.

BACK TO THE FUTURE

A lot of very impactful businesses have been built around technology that has existed for a long time. Personal assets are now being rented out. New technology-based "sharing" businesses are emerging to help people rent everything from homes (Airbnb) to cars (Turo) to even swimming pools (Swimply).

And that's the case for many of the "new" things right now. Airbnb has web technology that's been around for years—the same scheduling programs that online travel booking sites have used for decades. They put that together with someone who has a spare room in their house and created a new business. There's an Uber-style service for people who own boats now, and there's a service that allows people to rent cars from one another. People are home sharing, renting their homes to one another for six months. Do you live in the Canary Islands but need to do business in Ohio for a while? Go on a home sharing service site and work something out. The same could happen with specialized equipment. Instead of having to rent a piece of equipment from a rental company, people can connect with other companies.

The next step will be for employers to embrace this trend in some fashion. Employee sharing could be an idea that works soon. Maybe I have an employee who wants to see the world. I could let her go to New Zealand, let's say, and work for a year for a company that does what I do but isn't a competitor in exchange for one of their employees. There would be a fee associated with what I would get, plus I'd get expanded knowledge from my employee's exposure to a different company and different culture. There are a lot of interesting capabilities as communications causes our world to shrink. There are condominium projects being built in certain locations specifically for people to live and work there because where they work has become a moot point for their employer.

To take advantage of all these possibilities, you have to be ready for change. It also requires quite a bit of trust, but people must earn trust every day. If you can't trust them, then you've hired the wrong people to begin with. Whether you hired the wrong person in the Philippines or you hired them in Philadelphia doesn't really matter. It's still the wrong hire.

Video-based services, such as telemedicine, have been brought forward at an accelerated pace, and I think we'll see more of that. The idea that services have to come from somebody in your local neighborhood—or even in your state or country—isn't the case anymore. I think we're blowing all that stuff up. Doctors already do consultations remotely with the help of cameras and shared video. You can call the heart specialist in the middle of your surgery and allow them to look inside the patient's body from a camera above the operating table. Doctors are able to monitor their patients remotely now from implants.

I think it's funny that people are looking for a version of the Jetsons' robot housekeeper, Rosie, to appear one day to take care of all our needs. We could put together a laundry list of robotic things we've been using for decades that we just take for granted—everything from dishwashers and garage door openers to windows that raise and lower in our cars. Millions of things are robotic in nature. They're going to all get cobbled together, just like Uber, into some droid-looking thing that puts lug nuts on the cars on the assembly line so some poor guy doesn't have to do that one thousand times a day. All it takes is being observant about human nature and how people react to and interact with their environment to identify what the next need, the next technological leap, might be.

EMBRACE CHANGE

The change that's going on around us is constant. It's ever-evolving, and it's accelerating. The speed at which things are moving is getting faster, and the amount of change is more prevalent. People need to embrace this concept, as well as the idea of being a lifelong learner.

It's crucial to recognize that the way we do things and the technology used today will evolve, and adaptation is necessary to stay relevant. It is important to constantly learn from and embrace the changes around us, whether related to technology or the processes and systems we use. Make it a point to look at obstacles and issues from different perspectives and evaluate your surroundings to determine how to make functions more efficient and conducive to current lifestyles. Never forget your purpose and allow it to lead you to new solutions and innovation, using various tools and resources to your advantage. As the technology revolution unfolds, it will reveal a very decentralized stack of information with the decision-making process in the middle—make the decision to stay current and knowledgeable.

Everything is new and wonderful—explore and learn. My hope is that when you finish this book, you pick up another and read some more. In other words, keep learning.

Key Takeaways

- Mobility will come to data management systems.
- Coordinating technology between work and personal devices will continue to be a challenge.
- Our ability to connect will continue to improve.
- There will likely be a trend of simplification in manufacturing.
- Most technological leaps will likely come from new ideas about how to use existing technology.

APPENDIX

SELECT ARTICLES BY STEVE K. RICHMOND

UNCOVERING THE TRUE COSTS OF IT INFRASTRUCTURE

By Steve Richmond
Published by Forbes Technology Council
Forbes, November 3, 2021

IN TODAY'S HIGH-TECH environment, the total cost of IT infrastructure needed to run a business can be astounding if not carefully managed. From significant upfront costs and maintenance requirements to hardware replacements, upgrades and utilities to run it, the budget set aside for your IT infrastructure has the potential to far exceed your original expectations and can complicate things for your business.

One common mistake that many companies make is comparing ongoing cloud subscription expenses to the initial cost of an on-premise system without considering the continuous cost of system maintenance and upgrading over the application's lifetime. The expense of running a server in-house can be too expensive and has several drawbacks. In a 2012 article on Wired.com, Gartner, Inc. even estimates that the annual cost of owning and managing software programs might be up to four times the initial purchase price.

It makes sense to consider all of your options to find a great IT solution that's going to work best for your company and your budget. Here, I've identified a few key points to consider when you price out your IT infrastructure so that you can stay on track and mitigate the risk of overspending.

BIG COSTS FOR AN ON-SITE DEPLOYMENT

On-premise deployments often come with a hefty price tag, and enterprises must pay for the design, development, and deployment of a new application system upfront before it can go live. According to Gartner, Inc., the deployment of a software application involves eight key areas that can lead to massive costs:

1. **Data centers.** Data centers consume vast amounts of electricity, and U.S. data centers were projected to consume approximately 73 billion kWh in 2020.

2. **Network and storage.** Whether the on-premises server is located in a closet or in a data center, there are big costs associated with its location.

3. **Physical servers.** Physical hardware requires regular upkeep, and someone has to make sure everything works and can fix things when they break. You're going to be paying big for maintenance, monitoring, security and auditing on a routine basis.

4. **Virtualization.** Creating complex computing environments will save money in the long run, but you're going to pay a lot out of pocket to get a system properly set up and maintained.

5. **Operating system.** Using an OS that is outdated can lead to performance drops, and using new software on old hardware can cause even more problems that are complicated to fix and costly.

6. **Databases.** On-premise databases tend to be expensive and can lock you into costly agreements and strict licensing terms with vendors.

7. **Application.** The in-house development of applications, along with their ongoing maintenance, requires significant resources and budgets to maintain and keep up-to-date.

8. **Data.** The amount of information you need to store, maintain and analyze will directly affect the amount you pay to keep it secure and on-hand.

When a corporate application is run entirely on-premise, all of these key areas are self-managed and are your responsibility to maintain. In a SaaS cloud delivery model, however, a trusted SaaS solution provider oversees seven out the eight key areas, while you just manage the data.

CONSIDERING THE CLOUD

With all of the costs of an on-premise deployment for your IT infrastructure, it makes sense to consider the cloud. More organizations are comparing cloud platform features, functionality and operational expenses against those of on-premise applications. In fact, according to an October 2021 Markets and Markets report, the global cloud computing market size is only expected to grow, from $445.3 billion in 2021 to $947.3 billion by 2065.

Cloud apps are cost-effective, adaptable and secure, allowing businesses to deploy products and services faster than before. You'll have no upfront hardware or software licensing costs, and you'll only have to pay for the services you use. In some cases, the savings can be tenfold.

Making the jump to the cloud isn't without its share of challenges, however. Transitioning from on-site infrastructure can raise additional security concerns, though these issues are being addressed as technology advances and improves. Also, failing to have a well-thought-out plan or a defined business goal can lead to the cloud migration process being held up in later phases, preventing companies from reaping many benefits and leading to unnecessary charges.

Careful planning can help address these cloud challenges and early deployments and has provided insight so that many companies and service providers can overcome some of these early hurdles that others have faced.

KEEP THE FUTURE IN MIND

The shift to cloud computing should only continue to accelerate into the future. Cloud computing has been one of the most significant technological trends in recent years, and according to Benjamin Pimentel's 2019 Business Insider article, traditional servers are projected to account for only 32% of all enterprise applications in 2022, down from 63% in 2019. Meanwhile, cloud adoption and opportunities are expected to expand even further, leading to a $1 trillion market by 2024, according to Business Wire. Still, identifying all infrastructure components, business processes and available in-house knowledge is critical in establishing a strategy that addresses all of your organization's needs.

Even though it may seem like it would cost more to implement the best and latest IT infrastructure frameworks, it might be the best way for you to cut costs and enhance your business at the same time. Be sure to consider all of your options as you uncover the real costs behind your current IT solution.

JOINING FORCES: THREE THINGS TO CONSIDER WHEN PARTNERING FOR SUCCESS

By Steve Richmond
Published by Forbes Technology Council

Forbes, June 30, 2021

ONE THING I'VE found to be true is that no one is successful all on their own. Whether they have a strong team behind them, or they collaborate with others outside their organization to get the job done, every leader depends on others in some way to grow, learn and achieve their goals. No matter what line of work or industry you're in, the time will come when you have to decide if forging partnerships with other companies will help propel your business forward.

Sometimes, you'll be asked to partner with other companies to ensure the success of both businesses. One survey showed respondents reported up to 70% of business partnerships don't work out. However, I've always believed that establishing business partnerships is one of the most important steps you can take to grow, learn and ultimately surpass your expectations of what's possible. When looking to partner with others, there are a few things that I always take the time to consider, and I've found that whenever

I follow these guidelines, I end up with strong partnerships that really stand the test of time.

TAKE THE TIME TO CHOOSE

This is one of the most important actions you can take when starting a new partnership. First, you have to really consider who you want to partner with and why. You can start by creating a strategy on your own, and then start searching for who can best get you to where you want to be. In my own experience, I've chosen to team up with partners who can fulfill different aspects and lines of work that my own business isn't set up to fully carry out on its own.

This decision-making process will also require you to dedicate an ample amount of time to finding the right partner. It can't be a hurried process, and rushing to the finish line will only make you lose sight of the need to build up a strong foundation for the partnership to stand on. Even when you think you've found the best possible partner, take more time to think about every possible outcome, and then make the decision with confidence once you've considered it as closely as possible.

ALWAYS BASE PARTNERSHIPS ON TRUST

Trust is perhaps the most essential building block for any partnership, be it in business or other aspects of your life. Some of my first partnerships were with people who I knew in the business world for over 20 years, and seeing how someone works over an extended period of time helps build a strong element of trust in your relationship with that person going forward.

You can start finding people you can trust by looking within your own network of people or past coworkers you've known for a long time and who have done work that speaks for itself. You'll already have a good idea of their reputation, and if you've done business with them in the past, even better. Relying on word-of-mouth and referrals is also integral to this process, and I guarantee you'll eventually find some of the best partners for the job if you always remember to look for those you can really trust.

DEFINE YOUR PARAMETERS

Finding out and defining certain parameters when looking for business partners is crucial to honing in on what's important. Even if the initial relationship is based on trust, potential partners have their own way of doing things and often have others working for them that you won't ever interact with or get to know personally. Choosing partners who have certain degrees, demonstrated industry expertise or valid certifications is a great way to set guidelines for what to look for and determine who's going to have the knowledge and expertise necessary for the job.

One helpful parameter I've found is to choose partners who have great qualifications and are constantly overseen or verified by external companies or mass brand partners. This definitely helps with quality control, which is often a big challenge when establishing business partnerships. No matter what parameters you define for your own decision-making process, make sure that you stick to them, and you might even find a great partner in someone you never expected.

Creating lasting business relationships and partnerships doesn't have to be a difficult process, but it does require you to consider the whole picture when it comes to your company's needs and your future goals for growth and development. I've found that the best benefit to having good business partnerships is that you can get even better results out of your company and can truly become an expert in your niche since you combine the minds and determination of others who also want to succeed. That's the reason why I continue to dedicate a lot of time to build these relationships and encourage others to do the same.

INCREASE AFFORDABILITY AND EFFICIENCY WITH CLOUD-BASED EAM SYSTEMS

By Steve Richmond
Published by *Machinery and Equipment MRO*
February 16, 2022

IT'S NEVER BEEN more important for companies to manage assets effectively in order to scale in the best way possible. Just having a better product or service is no longer adequate in today's world; organizations are now expected to develop their product better, faster, and cheaper, meaning they need to maximize the productivity of their assets and equipment to really succeed.

Companies are now faced with the choice between installing enterprise asset management (EAM) Cloud or EAM On-Premise systems with modern applications to reach these goals. It was only a decade ago when the most typical way to deploy an EAM system was through an on-site data center, but things have changed.

On-premises installations that are hosted and controlled internally by IT departments are now being outperformed by software-as-a-service (SaaS) and cloud-based alternatives. Most EAM technologies are now cloud-based

SaaS models, and they offer some significant advantages, especially when it comes to increasing affordability and efficiency.

AFFORDABILITY

Perhaps the best thing about an EAM Cloud system is the amount of money you can save upfront. Their minimal start-up costs also make cloud EAM apps popular with smaller businesses. Cloud-based SaaS models eliminate the need for upfront capital investments, and you only pay for what you use. They give you the freedom to scale up or down your service based on your monthly requirements, and you also get seamless automated software upgrades and backups.

On the other hand, on-premise systems require a significant initial expenditure because you must acquire and maintain the gear required to run the EAM software. You'll end up spending more in the long run, and these costs can add up quickly. If affordability is your focus, go with an EAM Cloud system for the most bang for your buck.

EFFICIENCY

In a side-by-side comparison for efficiency, an EAM Cloud system is going to be far more superior to an EAM On-Premise system. With SaaS or cloud-based EAM systems, upgrades are handled automatically by the vendor, enabling workers to do other tasks and effectively outsource the technical expertise required with EAM maintenance. Updates are also performed regularly by software providers to improve software stability typically over-night, which allows for as little disruption as possible.

With an on-premise system, you'll be faced with big challenges if your physical premise is ever damaged by a natural disaster or power loss, which is not a problem when you store critical EAM data in the cloud. Aside from having to spend time maintaining and troubleshooting expensive on-site hardware, an on-premise system also doesn't offer efficient capabilities for your maintenance staff to access asset data via the cloud from any device, anywhere, instead of having the data on a single computer.

Choosing the appropriate EAM for your business is no easy task. First and foremost, you must examine your organization's needs, finances, data, and scalability constraints. However, most companies are going to find more benefits from an EAM Cloud system, especially when it comes down to affordability and efficiency.

FIVE WAYS TO IMPROVE YOUR COMPANY'S CYBERSECURITY

By Steve Richmond
Published by Forbes Technology Council
Forbes, December 1, 2020

AS THE COVID-19 pandemic shows no sign of slowing down, many companies have resorted to remote work-from-home operations. The rapid growth of remote working has given rise to massive vulnerabilities in cybersecurity and increased security incidents.

This transition underlines a challenge that businesses have faced for decades: the lack of effective information security. In reality, the infrastructure and policies needed for remote work have been in place for a while—the true issue lies with vulnerability related to cybersecurity.

THE IMPORTANCE OF CYBERSECURITY AGILITY

There's a metaphor I like to use when discussing cybersecurity: the office was like a fortress when it came to security, everything easily protected from within its walls. However, when working remotely, that layer of safety is quickly eroded—anything and anyone can come in.

Most businesses were unprepared for the abrupt changes that came with working remotely: many employees, for example, are using at-home electronic devices that are not protected by IT antivirus software or firewalls. It was simple when everything was within the company's walls: employees had their computers and phones pre-installed with security by the necessary departments. Now, it's much more about protecting the little "tents" and "outposts," which include remote workers' smartphones and computers. This is the key reason that we need to think differently about security.

Without the security protection offered by the office structure—the metaphorical walls of the castle—businesses are more vulnerable to cyberattacks. The failure to keep up with software patches or to use a company's VPN can cause data interception over unprotected channels. In 2020, companies are exposed to breaches and fraud on an unprecedented scale.

Companies can strengthen their cybersecurity systems by taking these five steps:

1. **Evaluate the effectiveness of your company's current security measures.** Obtaining certification from the International Organization for Standardization (ISO) for information technology and security techniques provides current and future cloud service customers an independent assurance that demonstrates compliance with important confidentiality, integrity and security controls.

2. **Invest in a scalable, high-bandwidth network infrastructure.** Developing an infrastructure capable of providing enhanced security options for sensitive data and enterprise applications will allow employees to collaborate conveniently and securely—anytime, anywhere.

3. **Upgrade security protocol.** By implementing authentication factors such as two-factor authentication (2FA) and multi-factor authentication (MFA), your employees and their data will be much safer from potential attacks. By providing a more secure authentication method, it makes it more difficult for attackers to bypass this additional security layer.

4. **Organize a phishing training course.** This provides employees with knowledge about online safety, as well as metrics on how their internet behavior has changed and improved. These forms of training should be performed regularly to keep everybody up-to-date with current data infringement practices which will protect your IP and company data.

5. **Conduct phishing simulations within your company.** Send a message regularly that asks for secure information and monitor how many people are flagging that information. It is important to rate how well your team performs and continues to improve to show progress.

STAYING CURRENT WITH CYBERSECURITY CHANGES

As cybersecurity threats continue to change, each company's cybersecurity protection systems need to evolve with it. It is necessary to perform periodic assessments of staff readiness to identify areas of vulnerability and to assess if existing policies and training need to be modified. To encourage compliance, documenting the results of all assessments, and ensuring that employees act on any risk remediation recommendations is best practice.

Cybersecurity is everyone's responsibility, but even the most resilient companies need effective leadership. If a business leader takes cybersecurity seriously, it will permeate throughout the entire company and help build a culture of enhanced cybersecurity awareness.

In a period of increasing vulnerabilities and attacks, there has never been a better time for executive leadership to step up and create a strong culture of cybersecurity that encourages everyone to know what the right actions are to take.

ADDITIONAL RESOURCES

- Maximo® Online Resources & Education (MORE): moremaximo.com
- ReliabilityWeb.com: reliabilityweb.com
- Projetech SaaS versus Hosting: projetech.com/maas/saas-vs-hosting
- Bruno Portaluri (MaximoDev): bportaluri.com/mxloader

NOTES

CHAPTER 1

1. "How COVID-19 Has Pushed Companies over the Technology Tipping Point—and Transformed Business Forever," McKinsey & Company, October 5, 2020, https://www.mckinsey.com/business-functions/strategy-and-corporate-finance/our-insights/how-covid-19-has-pushed-companies-over-the-technology-tipping-point-and-transformed-business-forever.

CHAPTER 2

1. IBM, *Understanding the Impact and Value of Enterprise Asset Management*, April 2019, page 9.
2. IBM, *Understanding the Impact and Value of Enterprise Asset Management*, April 2019, page 9.
3. Alina Tugend, "The 3,000-Mile Oil Change Is Pretty Much History," *New York Times*, September 10, 2010, http://www.nytimes.com/2010/09/11/your-money/11shortcuts.html?pagewanted=all&_r=0.
4. Warren Brown, Clyde Neely, and Steven J. Rossi, "New Guidelines for Pressure Boundary and Bolted Joint Assembly," ASME, December 28, 2010, www.asme.org/engineering-topics/articles/pressure-vessels/new-guidelines-for-pressure-boundary.
5. Joanna Bailey, "Drones Help Korean Air Slash Plane Inspection Times by 60%," Simple Flying, December 17, 2021, https://simpleflying.com/korean-air-drone-swarm.
6. Adrianna Nine, "Elon Musk Thinks Optimus Robot Could Be Bigger than Tesla," ExtremeTech, April 25, 2022, https://www.extremetech.com/electronics/334526-elon-musk-thinks-optimus-robot-could-be-bigger-than-tesla.

CHAPTER 3

1. Helen Edwards and Dave Edwards, "How Tesla 'Shot Itself in the Foot' by Trying to Hyper-Automate Its Factory," *Quartz,* May 1, 2018, https://qz.com/1261214/how-exactly-tesla-shot-itself-in-the-foot-by-trying-to-hyper-automate-its-factory.

2. Maximo* Online Resources & Education (MORE) Community (website), accessed July 7, 2022, https://moremaximo.com/home.

3. "'No Patent Suit against People Who Use Our Tech in Good Faith:' Elon Musk," NDTV, World, Agence France-Presse, updated February 2, 2019, https://www.ndtv.com/world-news/elon-musk-releases-all-tesla-patents-to-help-save-the-earth-1986450.

4. Eric S. Raymond, "Open Source," *Encyclopedia Britannica Online,* s.v., accessed July 7, 2022, https://www.britannica.com/topic/open-source.

5. Todd Neely, "Farm Sues John Deere for Repair Rights," Progressive Farmer, January 13, 2022, https://www.dtnpf.com/agriculture/web/ag/equipment/article/2022/01/13/north-dakota-farm-sues-john-deere.

CHAPTER 4

1. Stephen R. Anderson, "How Many Languages Are There in the World?" Linguistic Society of America, https://www.linguisticsociety.org/content/how-many-languages-are-there-world.

2. "Watson at Work: Engineering," *iSpot.tv*, https://www.ispot.tv/ad/wIha/ibm-watson-watson-at-work-engineering.

CHAPTER 5

1. Steve Richmond, "What the Healthcare Industry Can Learn about Digitization from Elon Musk and EAM Leaders," Forbes Technology Council, *Forbes,* June 10, 2020, https://www.forbes.com/sites/forbestechcouncil/2020/06/10/what-the-healthcare-industry-can-learn-about-digitization-from-elon-musk-and-eam-leaders/?sh=1ea038723dde.

2. Jiayi Shen, et al., "Artificial Intelligence versus Clinicians in Disease Diagnosis: Systematic Review," *JMIR Medical Informatics* 7, no. 3 (July–September 2019), https://www.ncbi.nlm.nih.gov/pmc/articles/PMC6716335.

3. Xiaoxuan Liu, et al., "A Comparison of Deep Learning Performance against Health-Care Professionals in Detecting Diseases from Medical Imaging: A Systematic Review and Meta-Analysis," *The Lancet* 1, no. 6 (October 1, 2019), p. 1, https://doi.org/10.1016/S2589-7500(19)30123-2.

CHAPTER 6

1. Ian McCue, "Obsolete Inventory Guide: How to Identify, Manage & Avoid It," *Oracle NetSuite*, October 15, 2020, https://www.netsuite.com/portal/resource/ articles/inventory-management/obsolete-inventory.shtml.
2. Ian McCue, "Inventory Carrying Costs: What It Is & How to Calculate It," *Oracle NetSuite*, November 6, 2020, https://www.netsuite.com/portal/resource/articles/ inventory-management/inventory-carrying-costs.shtml.
3. Dave Wendland, "Minimizing Touch Points Can Save You Time and Reduce Expenses," Forbes Technology Council, *Forbes*, January 19, 2018, https://www. forbes.com/sites/forbesagencycouncil/2018/01/19/minimizing-touch-points-can- save-you-time-and-reduce-expenses/?sh=43b9181b20d8.
4. "New Research Finds Mobility 'App Gap' in Enterprise IT—According to Progress Software," *BusinessWire,* January 24, 2013, https://www.businesswire.com/news/ home/20130124005179/en/New-Research-Finds-Mobility-%E2%80%9CApp- Gap%E2%80%9D-in-Enterprise-IT-%E2%80%93-According-to-Progress- Software.

CHAPTER 8

1. Ferry Grijpink, Alexandre Ménard, Halldor Sigurdsson, and Nemanja Vucevic, "The Road to 5G: The Inevitable Growth of Infrastructure Cost," McKinsey & Company, February 23, 2018, https://www.mckinsey.com/ industries/technology-media-and-telecommunications/our-insights/ the-road-to-5g-the-inevitable-growth-of-infrastructure-cost.
2. Bob Nielsen, "Historical Corn Grain Yields in the U.S.," *Pest & Crop Newsletter*, Purdue University, April 28, 2020, https://extension.entm.purdue.edu/newsletters/ pestandcrop/article/historical-corn-grain-yields-in-the-u-s/.
3. Mickey Herskowitz, "Dome Hits 30," *The Houston Post*, April 9, 1995, https:// www.astrosdaily.com/history/housing/h-dome30.html.

CHAPTER 9

1. Bill Gates, *Business @ the Speed of Thought: Succeeding in the Digital Economy* (New York: Warner Books, 1999).
2. "Moore's Law," *Encyclopedia Britannica Online*, s.v., accessed July 7, 2022, https:// www.britannica.com/technology/Moores-law.
3. "Metcalfe's Law," *Techopedia,* s.v., updated May 28, 2019, https://www.techopedia. com/definition/29066/metcalfes-law.
4. "Gartner Says Bring Your Own PC Security Will Transform Businesses within the Next Five Years," Gartner Inc. Newsroom, August 26, 2020, https://www.gartner.com/en/newsroom/ press-releases/2020-08-26-gartner-says-bring-your-own-pc-security-will-transfor.

ABOUT THE AUTHOR

STEVE K. RICHMOND is the founder of Projetech Inc, the most experienced provider of Maximo as a Service (MaaS) in the world. He was educated at the University of Cincinnati and embarked on a career in the mechanical contracting business.

Steve has more than thirty years of expertise in the field. He propelled Projetech from a small consultant-based organization that pioneered IBM MaaS in 1999 to its status today as a globally recognized MaaS provider. Projetech currently leads the category as an award-winning IBM Business Partner, among many other industry accolades.

Steve is an official member of the Forbes Technology Council, a published author, and an experienced speaker recognized in the industry. He is also an active advisor to the Galanthus Partners board, where he continues to push forward the concept of Maximo as a Service.

Steve currently spends his time with his family and dogs in his homes in Ohio and Florida.

www.ingramcontent.com/pod-product-compliance
Lightning Source LLC
Chambersburg PA
CBHW031856200326
41597CB00012B/435